Contents

Turning Terrible into Terrific

Changing Your Life
at the Speed of Thought

Dennis Cummins

BTP Publishing
A Division of BTP Productions

To my wife Lisa and my children

Christopher and Lauren

Your support, inspiration and unconditional love

make having a terrific life so easy.

☺ ☺

Turning Terrible into Terrific

Changing Your Life
at the Speed of Thought

About this Book

What does terrible look like for you? I define terrible as anything that prevents you from being happy. Terrible comes in many forms. It could be as severe as the loss of a loved one or the pain and suffering from a debilitating illness. It could be as significant as losing your home, losing your job, or the breakup of a meaningful relationship.

More often than not, however, most terrible things in life are not nearly as dramatic. I'm talking about the little annoyances we face on a daily basis including: putting up with negative co-workers, getting stuck in traffic, spilling coffee on yourself, dealing with relatives that annoy the crap out of you, sitting next to a person on a plane who has decided to engage you in a marathon one-way dialogue, being overworked, feeling like there is never enough time, or running late all the time because you're overwhelmed. These less catastrophic events are just as (if not more) damaging because they are often swept under the rug, ignored or denied proper corrective attention, as they insidiously and cumulatively deny you the ability to have a Terrific life.

The goal of this book is to empower you to face any terrible situation – large or small – and find ways to create terrific outcomes for yourself.

And, how would you describe Terrific?

Online dictionaries use words like great, intense, extraordinarily good or excellent. I prefer to describe Terrific in more tangible terms. Terrific means things are going your way; the events and circumstances of your life are in alignment with your desires. In other words, you're pretty darn happy about life. You look forward to each day and to what life will bring. You live a life filled with purpose, joy and pleasure.

Ideally, every one on the planet can live a terrific, happy life. But don't go filling your head with visions of sugarplums and lollipops. Instead, before you get all carried away thinking this book holds all the answers to your visions and thoughts of a utopian society in which your every desire is catered to, I want you to do one thing... Wake up! You live in the real world, not in a fairy tale. This book is not a magic lamp that can produce a genie when you rub it. I do not promise it supplies all the answers. However, keep reading and you will find it acts as the road map for you to take positive action in order to make permanent changes in your life, allowing you to turn any situation from terrible into terrific.

You don't need anyone to help you with the lessons you learn when things go right. But wouldn't it be great to have someone there to help you get through the times when things don't go right - the tough times, the hard times, the terrible times?

Better yet, wouldn't it be great to have someone teach you how to have fewer terrible times? And when you do have them, wouldn't it be nice to have some tools to get through them as quickly and as easily as possible?

You can do anything you set your mind to, if you're willing to do some work.

In my life, I have made great decisions and terrible ones. I have been presented with opportunity and with hardship. I have had great fortune and misfortune. I've also managed to celebrate the wins and learn from my losses.

So, why write a book?

For years I've watched and listened to people express how terrible their lives were. I've also watched the vast majority continue to do the same thing over and over again, despite the fact that their actions were the very cause of their unhappiness. I figured it was time to share the ideas and strategies that helped me turn my life around.

I wrote *Turning Terrible into Terrific* for several reasons. First and foremost I wrote it to make your life easier. It was written to bring more fun, more laughter, more joy, and more prosperity into your life. Secondly, I admit, I am among the more than 200 million people who wish to be published and this book allows me to accomplish that while helping others in a more exponential way. It allows me to reach a wider audience as well as expand my platform for future speaking engagements and workshops so I may continue to make a positive difference in peoples' lives.

I want to be up front with you from the start. By my reckoning, Plato and Aristotle are just about the only two original authors – of <u>everything</u>. Everyone else has been borrowing from them for a couple of dozen centuries. Anyone who claims otherwise about the contents of this book or any other book is full of.... misconceptions (I bet you thought I was going to say crap, didn't you?). So, there is probably not much in the way of original information in this book. However, the information in *Turning Terrible into Terrific* is presented in a practical, easily digestible way, based on real world results. It is presented in a way that is easy to understand and easy to implement. I offer tools to enable you to change your life at the speed of thought. * Warning * -- in so doing, I will most likely poke the part of your brain and your heart that needs to be awakened the most, whether you like it or not.

Turning your life from terrible into terrific is simple, if you know how.

In this book, I show you how.

Before You Get Started –
<u>Download your Guidebook and Bonus!</u>

Whether you purchased, won or were given this book – Congratulations!

Turning Terrible into Terrific it is an investment in your Self. It also comes with several gifts. Simply go to:

DENNISCUMMINS.COM/GIFT/

The first gift is **The Guidebook** for *Turning Terrible into Terrific.* You'll want to download the guidebook <u>before</u> you go any further. It provides the opportunity and structure for you to take immediate action during the exercises.

Let's face it; any activity is easier when you have someone to show you how it's done. Therefore, Dennis has created a T2T (*Turning Terrible into Terrific*) membership website. Inside the site you will find several tools designed to assist you in continuing your transformation beyond the experience of reading the book.

Go to: DENNISCUMMINS.COM/GIFT/
access the T2T membership site – FREE!

Why not let the T2T membership site act as your mentor? Along with the tools from this book it can assist you in having a life filled with abundant joy and success.

Moment of Decision

When my son was 15 years old, I attended his annual piano recital. It was truly amazing to see all the kids playing their hearts out on stage. For many of them, this was the first time they had ever played in front a large group of people. They all did a wonderful job.

One young man in particular struck me as noteworthy. It seemed he was new to playing the piano. As his name was called, he walked to the center of the stage. His head was down. In a mumbled voice he announced his name and the name of the song he was going to play. He then shuffled his way to the piano and fumbled with his sheet music.

I wriggled in my seat and leaned forward; curious to see how he would get through this. The boy began his piece, timidly striking each key. The pace of the music seemed a bit slow but overall he was doing a good job.

I sat back in my seat, as the young man seemed to become more comfortable.

About 45 seconds into the piece, the music suddenly stopped. The boy stared down. His face contorted as he looked at his fingers looming over the row of black and white ivory. With a furrowed brow, he seemed to be searching. He took his left hand off the piano and wiped his forehead. Even from eight rows back, I could see his hands were shaking.

Seconds ticked by, but I knew it must have felt like an eternity from stage. I silently rooted for this young man, realizing I was witnessing his personal *Moment of Decision.* I wondered what he would do – play or walk away?

> "In any moment of decision, the best thing you can do is the right thing, the next best thing is the wrong thing, and the worst thing you can do is nothing."
> Theodore Roosevelt

He chose to play.

I watched him close his eyes for a moment. When he re-opened them, he wiped both hands on his cleanly pressed black pants, returned them to their position above the keys and he blasted through what turned out to be a terrific (and virtually flawless) performance.

The entire room stood, clapping and cheering for what would be the highlight performance of the evening (except of course for my son's).

Imagine how great this young man must have felt for having the courage to continue and for the accolades he received after his performance. In the end, it turned out the boy had been playing piano for several years, but suffered such terrible stage fright he had been unwilling to appear before a live audience. His teacher had encouraged him to try and had coached him on what to do if he got stuck. Apparently it worked.

> "Most of the important things in the world have been accomplished by people who have kept on trying when there seemed to be no help at all."
> Dale Carnegie

In life we are often faced with *Moments of Decision*. Invariably the quality of life we live is directly related to the choices we make at those moments.

Imagine if that young man had decided to stop and give up. How do you think he would have felt about himself then? Disappointed. Perhaps, a failure.

When we choose *not* to move forward – we often label ourselves as a failure or we simply give excuses and bury our heads in the sand of denial. We stifle ourselves and in so doing we deprive others the opportunity of sharing our gifts.

Given the chance, I believe we all want to feel good about ourselves, to build our self-esteem. The only thing stopping us from have that feeling is the unwillingness to make the tough choices.

You are now at a *Moment of Decision*. What kind of future do you want for yourself? If you are willing to move forward in making the tough choices, are open to the possibility of new techniques and are willing to do the work it takes to get there, you will gain the ability to create whatever you desire for your future.

> "It is in your moments of decision that your destiny is shaped."
>
> Tony Robbins

Life is filled with *Moments of Decision.*
Make the tough choices.
The quality of life you lead is directly related to the choices you make.

A Patient in Denial becomes
the Answer for Those with Chronic Illness

I arrived at the emergency room on my 26th birthday feeling emotionally and physically defeated. I sat up on the exam table wincing in pain. The slightest movement felt like a knife stabbing into my gut.

I had ignored my body for eight months. I'd been in denial, following a diagnosis of Crohn's Disease – an insidious, life threatening auto-immune disease that attacks the intestines, affects the joints and eyes.

It also often takes lives.

The attending GI specialist looked at my pale, drawn face and gaunt 5'8", 99-pound slumped-over body and said, "Cathy, I am checking you into the hospital." The pain was unbearable. I wanted to protest, but all I could manage was a slight sigh as my head fell back onto the stark white gurney.

The physician informed my mother and two sisters that if I did not have emergency surgery, my intestines would perforate and I would most likely die. Seven hours later, I was wheeled back into the recovery room.

Drugged up on morphine and still doubled-over in pain, I made a decision as the nurses pumped me with even stronger medicine. I decided this was NOT the way I was going to spend the rest of my life. I slipped into unconsciousness determined to live.

Complications from the surgery led to more surgery, which led to more complications and additional treatment and recovery. In the end, it took two years, seven surgeries and months of rehabilitation to repair my weakened body.

I have never asked myself why this happened to me. I did ask myself, "What is it I am supposed to learn from this?"

Western Medicine saved me, for which I am grateful. However, it also almost killed me multiple times, too. I made the decision to find a better way.

I obviously needed a huge dose of reality, or as I call it 'a sledge-hammer', to put me on the right path. I am eternally grateful for my experience. I refused to allow this illness to define me. I was determined to heal my self and heal my life.

Acupuncture helped me through my recovery, but I realized that the physical, spiritual, and emotional all have to be healed, truly healed. I proceeded to take thousands of hours of training in all areas of energy medicine and healing arts. I was driven by all the people that did not get well, and I decided it was my mission to help people, before they ever got to the state I had gotten to back when I was a naïve 26-year-old faced with major health challenges.

Through holistic medicine and as an acupuncturist for the past 25 years, I have had the amazing fortune to help thousands of people rise from the trenches of suffering from chronic illness. My biggest commitment to my patients is maintaining a 'never give up' attitude. They know I understand what they are going through. They also know I am committed because it is holistic medicine that truly saved my life.

Cathy Goldstein – AP, Speaker, Educator

www.YourHealthUpfront.com/blog

Winners and Whiners

Have you ever noticed there are people who complain a lot? In fact, some people actually seem to thrive on complaining.

Have you ever been around someone who complains all the time? I'd be shocked if you haven't.

Complaining and whining seem to be a fairly universal trait in society these days. And there is a reason for that. Complaining absolves a person of responsibility for the things that aren't going well in his or her life.

The very act of complaining indicates that something or someone didn't act the way you thought they *should* have or *could* have. By complaining about things that don't go your way you make someone or something else responsible for what has happened to you. You've now become a victim. A victim of the economy, a victim of government, a victim of your spouse, a victim of your friends and relatives, a victim of the stock market, a victim of the education system that didn't prepare you for real life, and a victim of the countless other things for which you've complained.

> "If you have time to whine and complain about something then you have the time to do something about it."
>
> Anthony J. D'Angelo

Are You Being a Whiner?

Ask yourself this question, "Why do I complain?" People rarely continue to do something that has no payoff. The next question that needs to be asked is: "What's the payoff for complaining?" I think it basically boils down to two primary outcomes: attention and self-esteem.

Whiners thrive on the attention they ultimately get from their nasally complaints. It doesn't matter that the attention is negatively driven. In order to falsely elevate their self-esteem, they must whine their way through life so they do not feel so alone.

Most people go through life believing that there are some things they are simply stuck with. They live into their situation. It is their personal cross to bear. These people love to point out just how terrible life is. They attract bad situations like flowers attract bees. They are basically living disaster magnets.

These people have their own version of Murphy's Law. Murphy's Law states that whatever can go wrong will go wrong and usually at the worst time. The whiner's version goes one step further: Whatever can go wrong will go wrong and usually at the worst time and it will always happen to them.

These people expect to get stuck in traffic. They expect to have their food order be messed up at the restaurant. They expect their flight to be delayed or cancelled. They expect to be underpaid and under-appreciated at work. They expect to be overworked, overstressed, overtaxed, and under-acknowledged.

And they are because they choose to be.

No one is any better or worse than anyone else based on his or her suffering. We are all unique human beings with our own unique gifts. Every single person on the face of the earth is equally deserving of happiness, success and prosperity.

Does any of this resonate with you? Choosing to continue to suffer doesn't make you a better person or a nobler person. It just makes you an unhappy and unfulfilled person.

In fact, complaining actually leads to more suffering and dis-ease. When it comes right down to it, everything in life is about choice.

What are you choosing? Look around. Look at your life. Look at your financial statement. Look at your home. Look at the car you drive. Look at the places you eat, where you vacation, where you work. If you work for yourself, look at the type of work you do.

Are you happy with the answers? If so: good for you. If not, there are some choices for you to make. You may choose to keep the status quo or choose to change.

Ask yourself, "Why am I choosing what I am choosing?" People very rarely consciously choose something that is painful or uncomfortable for no reason. Let's face it, given the choice, would you rather choose pain and suffering or joy and happiness? Of course you'd choose the latter. No one would choose pain and suffering, unless there was a reason for it. A payoff, if you will. So what's your payoff for being unhappy?

For most people the reason is simple. Their fear of change is greater than the pain of their current lifestyle. Most people unfortunately go through life 'comfortably miserable'. They are unhappy – just not unhappy enough to do anything about it.

Another reason people continue to choose to be 'comfortably miserable' is that they don't feel they deserve to have the good things in life. They live their lives governed by a self-imposed set of limitations, often learned from their parents or teachers.

No matter what the reason, it all comes down to the choices you make. At any point in time you make a choice. The decisions you make are based on your past experiences and future expectations. The more often you make the same type of decision the more that type of decision-making becomes a habit.

As long as you continue to blame something or someone else for what has happened in your life, your ability to deliberately create happiness will be non-existent.

> "Instead of complaining that the rosebush is full of thorns, be happy that the thorn bush has roses."
> - Proverb

Think about it. The only reason you complain is because you are not happy. If you are complaining it can only be because you put yourself in a situation or condition of disappointment. Then you complained how it wasn't your fault. If you are like most people you continue to do the very thing you complain about over and over again. You are a professional whiner; the consummate complainer. Therefore, things are not all that terrific in your life.

Here's a bit of wisdom: No one likes a whiner!

The whiners were the kids that you wanted to beat up in high school. Or maybe you were that kid. Maybe you still are that kid. The only difference is you are not in high school anymore and there's no one around to beat you up.

That's too bad. You probably deserve a good beating!

However, in the absence of the class bully you've decided to do it to yourself. You beat yourself up by giving away your power and your ability to change your condition every time you whine and complain.

If you want to change anything in your life, if you want to turn something from terrible into terrific, you first need to acknowledge – You are in control. You will need to acknowledge that the situations you are currently in, both good and bad, are your choice.

I can read your mind. I can hear you whining to yourself right now. You are convincing yourself that this can't be true. After all you are not in control of everything in your environment. You may be an employee with a terrible boss or have relatives that drive you nuts. Right now your inner whiner is convincing you that there are some things that you just can't control.

In response to that, I would like to quote the ancient Greek philosopher Bullshiticus when he said, "What a load of crapola!"

Now, don't get me wrong. I never said that you could control your environment. I said that the key to your own personal power, the key to turning anything terrible into something terrific, is to realize that you control the most important piece of the situation – You.

It is never the situation that controls the outcome. The outcome of any situation is dependent on how you respond to it.

If you want to turn your life or any part of it from terrible into terrific, you must start here. Realize, you have the power to change.

Maybe you have a horrible boss. Most people believe there is nothing they can do. Wrong! Sure there is. You can kill them (not recommended) or you could quit (also not recommended, unless you have a game plan). Or here's a wild idea: you could figure out what makes him or her tick. Perhaps you could decide to become so amazingly invaluable that your boss becomes your biggest supporter. In the process you go from whiner to winner and your job goes from terrible to terrific.

Maybe you're in a terrible relationship. Maybe you're no longer happy with your partner. Perhaps you feel stuck and don't see a way out. But, there is. You can kill them (not recommended), you could get a divorce (also not recommended, unless you have a game plan), or here's a wild idea: you could sit down with your partner and ask them what they need from you in the relationship. Then, let them know what you need. Now you're ready to formulate a plan to make each other happier. You may have attempted this a thousand times before, but this time you can leave the whining, moaning and complaining at the door. Even if your partner hasn't broken this habit, you can. This may sound simplistic and it's not always the easiest way to go, but it beats the alternative: silently suffering.

Relationships (like everything else in the world) are subject to the laws of entropy. The law of entropy states that if left alone things eventually decay from a state of higher order and functionality to a state of lower order and chaos. For the purpose of this example it basically means: if you ignore your partner long enough your relationship is headed for the crapper.

On the other hand, in the process of working on your relationship you will either nurture and solidify it or know for sure that it is time to split. I once heard a phrase; "Sometimes you must let go of something good to make room for something great." Either way, you go from whiner to winner and your life starts to go from terrible to terrific.

> "In trying to get our own way, we should remember that kisses are sweeter than whine."
>
> Author Unknown

The Power of Perspective

A few years ago my wife Lisa and I went on a vacation with our two children to the Caribbean islands of Turks and Caicos. Our children, Christopher and Lauren, were seven and five at the time. When I booked the trip I booked us into one large hotel room, which usually worked out great for us.

Just before leaving, Lauren started to come down with a flu-like bug and I realized that we could use an extra bedroom so she could get rest when the rest of us were still in the room. Upon arrival at the resort, I asked the reception desk if they had any two-bedroom suites available. It was high season and the resort was quite full, but she informed me they had an oceanfront suite coming available later that afternoon and we could use our current room until then.

We had a crap load of luggage and I for one did not want to go through the process of packing and unpacking any more than needed. With the expectation of moving, we chose not to unpack. Plus, I wanted to hightail it to the pool and get this vacation started.

I dug out our bathing suits. After a quick-change we headed toward some chaise lounges, near the giant twisting water slides. After several hours of rigorous climbing, swooshing and splashing, the kids and my wife rested in the sun, while I checked with the desk to see if our room was ready. I was told the room would not be ready until later that evening.

I headed back to the family, slightly frustrated.

Evening rolled around. After dinner I checked back with the desk. Bad news. The room was not going to be ready until the morning. I walked away more than frustrated. My blood was beginning to boil a bit. The seeds of anger were beginning to sprout. But, I figured the end was in sight and pushed it away, choosing to focus on getting a good night's rest.

I headed back to the room. After telling the family we'd be staying there for the night, I rummaged through all the bags until I found the toothbrushes, toiletries, and pajamas. Meanwhile, I managed to keep everyone relatively calm and the grumbling to a minimum. Lauren was a bit cranky and irritable from not feeling well, but she was laughing by the time she lay her head down for the night.

The following morning I was standing at the front desk at 10:00 a.m., expecting to be handed the keys to our new suite. Again, I was told the room had not been vacated and it would most likely be available by noon.

I walked back to the room to let Lisa and the kids know that we would not be moving yet. Still not unpacked and into the second day of our trip, my pissed-off factor shot up a great big stalk and some buds. I was pissed at the hotel. I was pissed at the people who didn't vacate the room and I was pissed at everyone in my family for packing so much crap. Now I was stuck digging through it *again* to find more dry clothes and new bathing suits.

Noon rolled around and I strutted into the lobby, making a beeline for the reception desk. The clerk knew me by name at this point and said; "Good afternoon Mr. Cummins." He then proceeded to inform me the room would not be ready until 2:00 p.m.

After a heated, highly audible and irritable reply, I stomped out of the lobby toward the pool where Lisa and the kids were floating around on rafts and riding the slide.

I was completely exasperated. I was furious with the hotel, the staff, and the people that hadn't vacated the room I had been promised. I was annoyed that we were still stuck in the single room. I was angry that we were still living out of the unpacked luggage and ticked about the volume of crap we had packed. Basically, I just wanted to scream!

I was half way back to the pool when it hit me! I literally stopped in my tracks. I turned in a full circle and looked around.

It was beautiful. The entire resort property was landscaped with exotic flowers. The fragrant scents mixed with the subtle hint of a sea breeze were intoxicating. From where I was standing, I overlooked one of the most amazing white sandy beaches in all of the Caribbean. I was in the middle of paradise.

In that instant, I chose to think differently. I no longer blamed anyone for our situation. In an instant, I decided to be happy. I made the choice to be happy.

In that moment the stress left my shoulders, my gait slowed, the smile returned to my face, the tightness around my chest released, and I was truly happy.

On my way back to the pool I realized how foolish I had been. I had wasted almost two days in paradise whining and complaining instead of taking responsibility for my decisions and for my response to those decisions.

After all, I am the one who booked a single room. I am the one who packed all the stuff in the suitcases. I am also the one who decided not to unpack while we waited. Most importantly, I am the one that chose to allow those factors to affect my mood. I realized that once I took control and owned my decisions, I was able to be happy because I chose to be.

> "If you don't like something, change it. If you can't change it, change your attitude."
>
> Maya Angelou

Choose to Be a Winner

How do you become a winner? Choose. Choose to look at your life's past, present and future – differently.

Stop complaining. Stop whining. Stop blaming. Stop justifying.

How do you do this? Easy! It's called re-framing. See, for every negative there is a positive. For every in-action there is an action that can be taken to improve a given situation. Re-framing is utilizing perspective to change a negative into a positive and it is as simple as changing the language you use.

"A winner never whines."

Paul Brown

In order to stop whining and complaining you must first change the words you use in describing everyday things. I realize it may require you to actually stretch your vocabulary a bit, but I assure you, it will be worth the effort.

These days certain harmful words are over-used to poorly describe what is actually happening in our lives. Profanity is a solid example of this. Misused as filler to describe any number of situations, profanity is the easy way out in verbalizing one's emotions. I urge you to choose to dig deeper and really express yourself rather than hiding behind the four-letter words that are strewn around so easily these days. Sure, we've all had our moments – so I'll refrain from unnecessary examples. However, these should be the exception rather than the norm. The prolific use of profanity simply sinks you down to a lower level and dilutes your argument rather than enhance it. Intelligence always trumps profanity.

Another over-used and equally dangerous word is HATE. It's another common filler used to describe the simplest of situations or tasks. Seriously, do you really *hate* the sun in your eyes? Does it actually cause you to have so much disdain for the sun that it evokes hostility or animosity toward an inanimate object? I doubt it. In all actuality, having the sun in your eyes simply irritates you because it's more difficult to see and you don't like having to squint. Do you really *hate* when someone mispronounces your name? Does it cause you to have anger or animosity toward the person who made the mistake? Seriously, are you going to let something as simple as that raise your blood pressure to the point of causing a heart attack? I hope not, but I do hope you get my point.

These descriptions of emotions are the definition of the word hate. And whether you believe it or not, words have power. Your misuse of this word gives the word power over you.

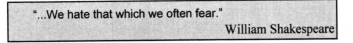

"...We hate that which we often fear."
William Shakespeare

My suggestion: Just like we say with small children - use your words. Exercise your vocabulary. No, that does not mean using even more colorful expletives. (Very funny, I can't even print most of the words you are thinking of right now). Get the point. Say what you truly mean and mean what you say.

Another way of re-framing is the use of positive descriptions rather than using negative words such as 'no' or 'not'. The brain only processes in positives. In other words, when you make statements like "I don't like rain" the brain processes "I like rain".

If you listen to Winners, you'll notice they typically speak in positive voice and when Winners lose, they continue to take responsibility for their actions while praising the actions of their competitor. Look at any great tennis pro or golf pro, professional swimmer, or baseball player. (No, I am not talking about the select few over-the-top attention seekers out there whose personas are predicated on them being obnoxious.) They are Winners. They are simply great athletes, performers or professionals that know how to win.

Winners do not accept defeat. They learn from it and then they let it propel them. They do not give up. They do not bitch, moan or complain, and they definitely do not whine. Winners are not infallible. Instead, they choose to get up when they fall down, they ask for help, have coaches to improve their game and they surround themselves with other Winners. And yes, sometimes they get pissed off. But rather than sit around angry, they move on quickly. Their choices are solution-based. They figure out how to make a bad situation better, make a conscious decision to change and then take action.

Right now it is your chance to choose. You get to make a decision. A decision to put this book down or a decision to continue reading and facilitate change in your life.

Choose to be a Winner.

> "If you don't see yourself as a winner, then you cannot perform as a winner."
>
> Zig Ziglar

Words have meaning.
Quit whining. Stop complaining.
Change your perspective.
Choose to be a Winner.

Stop Feeling Sorry for Yourself

Glad you're still here. Great decision! Congratulations for making a choice that will move you forward. Now let's continue doing some of the hard work that will help life become easier in the long run.

One reason your life may not be as terrific as you would like it to be is because you are too attached to feeling sorry for yourself. Think about it: your thoughts lead to your feelings, which in turn lead to the actions you take in your life, which ultimately determine your results.

If you are in the mode of continuing to feel sorry for yourself, then your feelings will, on a conscious or subconscious level, lead you to take actions that create results that allow you to continue to feel sorry for yourself.

It's a self-perpetuating cycle. It has become a habit.

"Chains of habit are too light to be felt until they are too heavy to be broken."

Warren Buffett

You may be feeling sorry for yourself because you are choosing to focus either on your past or on your future. Stop. The past is just that – passed. Continuing to reflect or focus on your past will lead to thoughts of regret. Wishing you could turn back time, and do something differently can only keep you stuck. Stop going over it like a broken record. You cannot change what happened no matter how much you think about it. However, you can learn from it. Focus on finding the lesson. Choose to learn by making positive changes in your current situation that do not lead to repeating the patterns of the past.

On the contrary, if you focus too much on the future, you will do so to your detriment. Dreaming of what is to come does not assist you with your current situation. The future can be a guide or beacon, but you must have a plan for today in order for life to look the way you want it to tomorrow.

If your focus on the future is predicated upon fear or

dread, regarding what you believe may happen, then it absolutely will come true. Remember, what you focus on expands. So, if you focus on a bleak future, your future will be bleak.

Focusing on tomorrow is stifling; no matter what 'future picture' you are painting for yourself. It holds you back from enjoying the moment. Remember, it's important to make each day and every moment count.

> "One of the most tragic things I know about human nature is that all of us tend to put off living. We are all dreaming of some magical rose garden over the horizon instead of enjoying the roses that are blooming outside our windows today."
> Dale Carnegie

If you put all your focus on the past or the future, life can seem terrible. But if you focus on the *now*, and choose to make it terrific, it can be. The trick is to allow yourself to be happy in spite of what is going on around you. Eventually, the terrific moments add up. Like building blocks, these moments will begin to compound on themselves and soon your whole life becomes terrific, rather than just the separate parts. Remember, today is where you can choose to think positively, in every moment.

You can choose to be terrific. You can choose to break out from the holding pattern that is keeping you from having an extraordinary life.

In fact, why not choose to be wild! Be silly! Oh, you're not okay with being wild or silly?

I see. Well, you're no different than most people. Most people are afraid to be silly. They don't want to look foolish or weird. They get too hung up on what other people think. They're afraid of others' opinions. Does that sound terrific?

I say, be willing to look foolish. Who cares what other people think? Allow yourself to be silly. It might just be what those around you need <u>most</u>.

For example: I am a chiropractor, speaker and trainer, but I am also a dad. My biggest job as a dad is to make my daughter laugh (and she'll be the first to tell you this). She is my *Why* (my propelling force) and I relish any opportunity to make Lauren laugh on a regular basis.

Sometimes that means being wild, silly, and even weird in my role as a parent.

One of my absolute favorite ways to make my daughter laugh is taking her for a Deli-bration.

I can hear you already. "What the heck is a Deli-bration?" I am so glad you asked.

A Deli-bration

In our household, I am the one that enjoys cooking. Therefore, I also tend to do most of the shopping and my daughter Lauren *loves* to go grocery shopping with me. The moment she hears about the possibility of me heading to the local Stop & Shop, she anxiously awaits an invitation. Of course, I am happy to oblige. Once we arrive at the store, we head straight for the deli counter. I'll pull a ticket from the big red box, lean down and whisper the number in Lauren's ear then we both eagerly await our deli-bration.

Here is how it works. We pretend it's like a lottery. We compare our number with the one on the board and eagerly wait to see if (more like, when) our number will be called. And as we get closer and closer, the excitement builds!

To give you a better description: let's say we pulled the number 84 and the number on the wall reads 81. As the number changes to 82, I'll lean back down to Lauren and eagerly say, "Lauren, I think we're gonna win." She smiles back at me, rubbing her hands together. "Here we go," I'll continue, "82." By this time Lauren is all smiles and a giggle or two have popped out. Sometimes I'll hold her hand in anticipation. "Here we go, Lauren. Get ready. I think we're gonna win." She'll laugh and I'll stand up and say, "They're up to 83. We've almost got it."

As our number is called I'll scream, "Yes, 84! We did it. We're winners!" By this time I am jumping up and down and I'll shout, "WooHoo, I knew it. I knew it. I knew we were going to win!"

Now Lauren is belly-laughing so hard she can barely breathe and my howling has everyone in the corner of the supermarket staring at us. The people behind the counter are clapping and everyone has a smile on their face, they're all laughing, too.

Is it silly? Yes. Is it odd? Absolutely. It's also incredibly fun and you watch how the energy, not just from my little girl, but also the entire back corner of a 10,000 square foot supermarket, is completely changed in that moment. That's how I know I am doing my job. Like I said, it's my job to make my daughter laugh.

Go ahead. Be silly, be wild, and have fun.

> "What fun is it being cool if you can't wear a sombrero?"
> Calvin & Hobbes

As I mentioned, my inspiration for being wild and silly is my daughter Lauren. At this time I'd love to share a little bit about the reason why. You see, Lauren is thirteen-years-old and she is unreasonably happy. She is also unstoppable; especially when it comes to talking to everyone she meets. She is a social butterfly with an uncanny ability to make friends instantly and permanently. When she walks into a room people seem to be attracted to her. She's like a little happiness vending machine. She thrives on cheering people up when they are sad or not feeling well. She is tall and slender. She has a beautiful head of thick light-brown hair, which she gets from her mother's side of the family. She also has a great sense of humor. She gets that from me.

The most striking thing about Lauren is the color of her eyes. Just about everyone that meets her says that she has the most incredible blue eyes they've ever seen. And I have to agree with them. But there is something about Lauren's eyes most people don't notice right away. They don't work. You see... my daughter is blind.

At the age of two Lauren was diagnosed with a brain tumor that has caused her to lose her vision. Over the last 11 years, Lauren's world has gone from blurry to black. She has been sickened by three separate courses of chemotherapy and has had over 25 major surgeries.

Over the last 11 years, Lauren has been poked and prodded by more doctors than I can remember. She has been stabbed by more needles than anyone should experience in a lifetime and has lost most of the use of the right side of her body. And over the last 11 years, Lauren has <u>never</u> felt sorry for herself. Never once whined or complained about the way things are.

See, Lauren chooses to be happy each and every day, and her happiness is contagious. However, I admit choosing to view life as terrific is not always as easy as heading out to the local grocery store and sharing a deli-bration.

In our family we choose to focus on our daughter as a whole, not the illness.

Yet, I am not infallible. There are times when I've felt a little down or depressed about the way things are in areas of my life, especially when it comes to Lauren. However, whenever I find myself in that space I immediately initiate 'Plan B'. When I do, everything instantly becomes okay.

What is 'Plan B'?

Good question. 'Plan B' is for those moments where you pull out all the stops to choose to see things differently. A last resort when you feel that things are starting to go terrible in your life. It is the only time I even remotely suggest comparing yourself to others and it is not to be used lightly.

> "Know that what you do in the time of your greatest trial can be your greatest triumph."
> Neale Donald Walsch

Think about someone who has it worse than you. Take a long hard look at their life and then say to yourself, "Now, that's really messed up!"

This is the one and only time I think of my daughter differently. I use her situation, not her Self, as a reminder to quit feeling sorry for myself. I use her illness to remind me of just how great I have it and I use her strength and amazing attitude to break me out of my bad mood.

Try it. If you don't know someone directly than look in your neighborhood, research a story on the Internet, or just listen to the news. There's bound to be someone in the spotlight that has it worse than you do. Think about their issue. Imagine for a second what it would be like to be them. You will probably find that it is hard to continue to throw yourself a pity party when you know someone else has it much worse than you do. And here's a bonus, if you really want to start to feel better about yourself and your current situation even faster, do something to help that other person. Stop thinking about what you can do for yourself and start thinking about what you can do for them. It will make both of you feel better.

> "Happiness comes when your work and words are of benefit to yourself and others... Set your heart on doing good. Do it over and over again, and you will be filled with joy."
>
> Buddha

Stop feeling sorry for yourself.
It's very unattractive. It's also selfish.
Instead, be silly. Be wild. Have fun.

What Love Has to Do with It

"...You are so messed up, clueless about what it takes to have a real relationship... You will NEVER have a healthy, long-term relationship. You will always mess it up, and you will die alone!" With that my girlfriend of three years stormed out of my life.

The words stung, but I figured she was just angry, bitter, and simply –wrong. Soon, I forgot about my ex-girlfriend, her venomous words and everything that had to do with our relationship. Eventually, I met another wonderful woman, fell in love and got married.

It was great in the beginning. However, we fought a lot. We went to a marriage counselor, read books on how to save our marriage. We even bought a house together. Inevitably, we decided to 'give the relationship some space'.

As a schoolteacher in New York City's South Bronx, I had the summers off. I decided to visit my brother in Northern California. By the time I returned home, I was faced with the hard reality that my marriage was over.

I began to drink almost every night. Those haunting words of my ex-girlfriend came back to me "you will die alone!"

I felt sorry for myself and ashamed at the mess I had created in my personal life. Then one night, something snapped. I cried out to the heavens, screamed for help and, with conviction, I decided I would find love. I deserved love. And I was willing to do whatever necessary to learn, grow and create the relationship I had always dreamed was possible.

In that moment, my feelings changed from despair to... hope.

I read relationship books, listened to CD's and made the decision to take responsibility for my part in my failed relationships while refusing to be defined by someone else. I also decided to stop feeling sorry for myself.

I knew it would take a massive change. I packed up my car and headed to Oakland, near San Francisco. I had no job, no connections, and strangely – no fears.

One year after landing in Oakland, I went out on my first date with Lara. More than a decade later, she still makes me swoon!

Today, we are happily married and we spend as much time together as possible. We have a beautiful daughter and attend every school play and function as a family.

I now understand what it takes to have healthy relationships and together, Lara and I are dedicated to helping others in attracting their soul mates.

We're just getting started and I am grateful for every second.

Johnny Fernandez
Co-creator of The Love Launch Weekend Seminar
LifeLaunchTraining.com

Finding Happiness

In the last chapter I urged you to stop feeling sorry for yourself and quit the darn pity party. I even suggested, if you can't manage to do it on your own, look at someone else's misfortune and use it as a propelling force to get out of your own doldrums. Yet, this does not mean I advocate 'comparison' as a primary motivator.

In fact, I urge you to actually stop looking at someone else's good fortune and comparing it to your own. Too often people look to what someone else has with a sense of wistfulness, regret or envy. They use others' successes as a bar for their own success... or lack thereof. It's unhealthy and in many cases will actually hold you back rather than propel you forward.

Don't get me wrong. I think it's critical to have goals and to strive for growth and development. But you know the expression 'The grass is always greener on the other side'? It's dangerous, if not plain dumb. It is okay to want more, but don't compare your situation with others. You never know the price someone has paid for the stellar situation they *seem* to be in.

Instead, I suggest you focus on what you have control over – your own happiness.

> "The Constitution only gives people the right to pursue happiness. You have to catch it yourself."
>
> Ben Franklin

Happiness by definition is a display of marked pleasure, satisfaction or joy. I suggest it's more of an indefinable feeling of elation marked by an outward smile or quite possibly an inward smile. It's when your heart is smiling, even when you may look stone-faced on a busy subway or in the midst of a serious business meeting. It's a state of being, sometimes calm and sometimes downright off the charts. Unlocking your happiness is ultimately the answer to *Turning Terrible into Terrific.*

Unfortunately, most people don't know how to find happiness. Instead, they allow happiness to roll in and out of their lives every once in a while, like the wind. They leave finding happiness up to chance.

Do you think happiness is out of your control? It's not. However, it does take action in order to live in happiness. It is a result of your efforts, not a chance encounter.

If you are ready to let go of whining, complaining and feeling sorry for yourself, you can intentionally have a happier, more terrific life.

There are 5 Keys to Happiness. They are quite simple (because I don't really see the need to make things complicated), yet require effort and practice in order to master.

The 5 Keys to Happiness

 Love what you have right now.

 Love where you live right now.

Love the people in your life right now.

Love yourself for who you are right now.

Have Gratitude – for everything good as well as for all the challenges, past and present.

Use all five keys, all the time, in every situation, and you'll have mastered the foundation for *Turning Terrible into Terrific*. Now it's time to move forward and take action on what you REALLY want.

Oh wait. Is that you I hear grumbling? You think this all sounds easier said than done? You're right. Sometimes it is easier said than done. I told you the five keys were simple. I never said they were easy. But, I can assure you; if you instill these five keys into your everyday life – your life will be terrific.

Ha. I can hear you now... "But Dennis, you don't understand. I..."

Oh, but I *do* understand. I've been there – wallowing in my own discomfort and misery regarding my surroundings; comparing my situation with others, feeling sorry for myself. Until the day everything changed for me.

The day I found my happiness...

With limited amounts of poor quality sleep and even worse food, my wife Lisa and I had been living in a noisy uncomfortable hospital, sleeping in a chair beside my only daughter for almost a week. Lauren had just undergone here sixth brain surgery and was lying in a semi-comatose state with a breathing tube attached to a ventilator, five separate IV lines delivering medications, and a catheter to catch her urine. Imagine being in that situation and still being grateful for all you have.

Lisa left the evening before to go uptown to the Ronald McDonald House to get a solid night of sleep. It was my sixth morning at the hospital. I had just spent another long restless night with Lauren. (Hospitals, in case you didn't know, are not exactly the best places to get rest and be comfortable.)

I had gone down the hall to the family shower area and had forgotten my shave gear. On my way back to the room, I noticed one of the floor nurses stopping the man with the meal cart. I watched as he nodded his head and move his cart out of the way. He then stepped to the side and waited as she wheeled a patient down the hall.

I thought it was a little unusual since the halls were definitely wide enough for them to pass.

I collected my razor and shave cream and was just about to head back to the shower when a serious looking nurse stopped me at the door and politely asked me to wait inside while they brought a patient down the hall. There was something strained about her demeanor.

I thought it was an odd request. My mind began to invent reasons for it. Perhaps it was a psychotic patient and they feared for our safety, perhaps the patient was bleeding and the nurses didn't want to frighten the other young patients, or perhaps the person on the gurney was contagious and they were worried about infection.

In the end, I theorized that the child must be female and that because of a cultural or a religious belief she could not be in the same area as a member of the opposite sex. In any event, I obediently stayed inside and waited by the door.

As the child was wheeled past our door I realized I had guessed wrong. I immediately understood why they wanted the halls cleared.

Judging by the patient's size, I guessed the child to be about the same age as my daughter Lauren. It was hard to tell for sure because he or she was completely covered with a white sheet. The child had passed away earlier that morning. In that moment, I said a prayer for the soul of that child and for their family... And in that moment, I chose to be EXTREMELY GRATEFUL for <u>everything</u> in my life including: the six surgeries, the ventilator tube, the five IV lines, the catheter, the sleepless nights, the crappy food, and most of all – for my baby girl Lauren.

* * *

There is no need for something this tragic to happen for you to incorporate The 5 Keys to Happiness into your life. Instead, why not simply choose to start right now.

This next section addresses each key individually and includes exercises to assist you in changing your mindset and implementing positive action into your life.

You may choose to read through them first or simply dive in and complete each exercise as you read it.

You will need a few things to get started:

1) <u>Your Guidebook</u> – If you aren't already using your guidebook, you may access it by going to:

DENNISCUMMINS.COM/GIFT/

If you are unable to download the guidebook, find a lined-spiral notebook or journal dedicated to the work from *Turning Terrible into Terrific*. For those of you who wish to use something fancier – go for it!

2) <u>A Pen or Pencil</u>.

3) <u>A smile</u> (This one is optional).

Love what you have right now.

We live in a fast-paced environment filled with new high-tech accessories coming out every day, upgrades available at every turn, and the latest-greatest-snazziestshiniest needs and wants advertised in every possible way. None of these 'things' have anything to do with long-lasting happiness. Now don't get me wrong, some of them may make life easier, more fun and bring a smile to your face, and may even give you a false sense of happiness for the moment. However, they don't create joy from within and until you appreciate what you have right now, no 'thing' in the world will sustain you.

They may mask the symptoms for a while, but they will not cure your unhappiness or your misery. In order to turn your life from terrible into terrific or good to great, you must first appreciate everything you have in your life right now.

This is the first key to happiness and in order to assist you in appreciating what you have right now, I've come up with a simple (not necessarily easy) exercise.

Appreciation Exercise

You will need your journal/notebook and a pen or pencil. This exercise is to be done in one sitting. Please allow at least 20 minutes to half an hour to complete it. (Stop grumbling).

At the top of the page write "I love what I have right now". Then, skipping every other line, list all the things you have right now. Write at least 100. Like I said, do it in one sitting. Write in <u>positive</u> <u>voice</u> only (this means positive wording). Refrain from words like no or not and write it with a smile (Yup, this time the smile is mandatory). Write tangible things, intangible things, big things and small things. Write.

<u>Example:</u>

I have a car that runs.

I have a healthy body.

I have a job.

I have healthy children.

I have a home filled with love.

I am smart.

I have a roof over my head.

I have the ability to collect unemployment while I am looking for work.

I have a mass transit system nearby to get where I need to go.

Etc., etc., etc.

See. That wasn't that hard. You have just listed things in gratitude and gratitude is where growth begins.

> "The roots of all goodness lie in the soil of appreciation for goodness."
>
> Dalai Lama

Love where you live right now.
The second key to happiness expands upon the last. Not the list, but the gratitude.

Whether you are renting, own, share, or simply have a room... love where you live right now. It is great to have a dream-home in your mind, on your vision board (If you don't know what a vision board is or have not done one, don't worry I will talk about vision boards in a later chapter). You may even pass by your dream-home each day to and from work or school. However, in order to reach for the goal of attaining your dream-home, you must first love where you live right now.

Respect your home. If it is messy – clean it up. If you have clutter – get rid of it. If the yard is a wreck – mow the lawn and manicure your space. Respecting your space is equivalent to respecting yourself. Remember, all of life is a mirror and if your home is out of alignment most likely so are you. Get your house in order and things will begin to fall into place.

An Exercise in Loving Your Home

1) <u>Take it one section at a time.</u> Decide on where to begin. For example, if a whole room needs cleaning up – tackle one thing at a time. Take it one drawer at a time.

2) <u>Use Time over Completion as a measure.</u> In other words, set aside a specific amount of time to tackle a project. Begin with half an hour and make sure the job is not so big that you make more of a mess than when you began. Example: if it is your desk that needs cleaning off – don't tackle the whole desk. Tackle one pile for half an hour. If you complete the task early – great! If there is still

more to do, you know where to begin during your next allotted time.

3) <u>Keep going.</u> If you schedule in the time at least once a week (how about at least an hour a week) and do it every week, you'll begin to build momentum and start to see results. Focus on the results rather than the task. Remember to celebrate your wins by enjoying your space. When your home is in order – it's much easier to love it no matter what the 'story' behind it is.

4) <u>Go the extra mile.</u> Cleanliness and organization is vital to respecting your home. However, if you really want to love where you live right now – show your home some love. It may be as simple as re-arranging some furniture, possibly painting the walls or buying a new plant or painting. When you love the space you live in, you'll feel even better about yourself.

Love the people in your life right now.

Sometimes easier said than done, this key is vital. If you choose to maintain a relationship with someone –

love them. It doesn't mean you have to agree with their beliefs, choices, or actions but it does mean you have to treat them with respect and kindness.

Love by my definition means to have concern for the good of another. To have strong affection for another based on kinship, personal ties, or romantic emotion. Nowhere does it say you must agree with the opinions or even like the actions of another. It also does not say you *must* love someone. It's a choice.

> "Being deeply loved by someone gives you strength, while loving someone deeply gives you courage."
>
> Lao Tzu

Are you loving others well? In other words do you offer joy, laughter, and are you dedicated to your collective goals? If the answer isn't a quick yes... it may be time for you to sit down and ask yourself, why not? Now, this isn't a moment for you to rattle off all the things you find wrong in another person or things that are out of your own control in a relationship. This is about you. If you find yourself in a place where you are questioning your love for someone; it's a good time for you to reflect upon how you may improve on loving that person, including answering one of the biggest questions, "How can I disagree and love him or her anyway?"

> "All love shifts and changes. I don't know if you can be wholeheartedly in love all the time."
>
> Julie Andrews

This is not simply for intimate relationships; it goes for all relationships in your life. Remember, everything is perception and perspective and it is seldom that yours will exactly match that of another. When communication breaks down, those divides become greater and greater. Egos get in the way and things begin to part even further. That is how a small incident can escalate into a full-out war in no time. Sometimes when this happens, you need to treat yourself as if you were a six-year-old. Give yourself a time-out. Find a respectful, neutral zone and ask for time to cool down. If you are not communicating well inside an argument than state your intention to cool down a bit. Without stating your intention, a disappearing act can be misunderstood. Increased misunderstanding will only lead to greater pain.

Unable to come to some kind of peaceful resolution or cool the situation down? Then the next step is to ask yourself – does this relationship serve me well? In other words, are you feeling fulfilled mentally, physically, emotionally, sexually (where it applies)? Now, hold on before you answer these. Don't be so quick to judge. Instead, really think about it. Look for the joy in the relationship, what has it meant to you, what did it look like when it was working really well.

Why did I ask you to take your time? Because when we are unhappy, angry or frustrated in a relationship, it's easy to head straight for the jugular of negativity when in fact this is a moment (or possibly cumulative moments) or a piece of the whole. It's important to look back upon the relationship and ask, "Was there a time when I felt fulfilled in this relationship?" If the answer is yes, even if that moment feels like it was far off in the distance, very long ago – there is a ray of sunshine here.

> "I have found the paradox, that if you love until it hurts, there can be no more hurt, only more love."
>
> Mother Theresa

Do not take this lightly. Too many relationships end pre-maturely because someone gives up too soon. Don't let that person be you.

How did it feel when you were completely fulfilled by this relationship? Physically? Emotionally? Spiritually? And if suitable, sexually? Can you remember a time, place, event or moment when this relationship truly served you well? When you felt utterly happy and content?

If yes, Fabulous. Work on re-building that connection. Re-establish and possibly even find new common ground to stand on in order to heal and move forward in a positive direction.

> "Fortune and love favor the brave."
>
> Ovid

However, if the answer is no – you have made every effort to improve things, or you've found that your value system is not compatible with the other person – there may come a time when you know in your heart that the relationship does not serve you well. If it's not serving you, it's probably not serving the other person either. If this is the case, you may not like what I have to say.

It may simply be time to move on.

Yes. I am suggesting it may be time for you to move on.

It may sound harsh. But, it's what I call – loving from afar. Now, you may be screaming in your head (or into this book), "But, Dennis I can't do that – they're family!" or "But I've known them all my life," or even, "But, she/he is my daughter/son."

I understand....

Move on.

If you are troubled by this suggestion – look back. Remember how I warned you to take your time before deciding if this relationship serves you well. Well, revisit your answer and your decision-making process. Is it healthy to stay in it? What positives can you pull from this relationship?

Can you name at least 10 things about this person that you are encouraged by? Not their potential, but rather who they are right now, in this moment. Come on, 10 things you admire or find wonderful in this person.

Found them? Now, build from there. Apparently, there is something to hold onto in this relationship, including taking a long, hard look at yourself and see if you can do some things to improve this relationship. I am sure there are.

However, if you can't find 10, try to find at least two or three. If you can't find at least something positive regarding this person, then my suggestion is this relationship may have run its course and it may simply be time to let go.

Before you start getting all upset at what I am saying – remember I didn't say stop loving them. You can love someone without having him or her in your life. In fact, sometimes we love better from afar. It doesn't mean you get angry or aggressive with them or even tell them you are extracting them from your life. Simply do it. Let the relationship or contact fizzle out naturally. If you stop giving this toxic relationship energy, it will either change or gradually dissipate. Either way – it's better for your own health and happiness and more often than not, it's better for the other person, too.

> "A big part of letting go is recognizing when it is time to stay in a situation and when it is time to move on."
>
> Darren L. Johnson

Love yourself for who you are right now.

It's amazing how many of you will have more trouble with this key than any other. Most people are their own harshest critics. Some people put more value on what others think of them than they do their own opinions of themselves. They've been beaten down by self-doubt or by the negative talk or abuse from others. Identifying your self-worth, finding your greatness and making a conscious effort to love yourself is vital to your happiness and success.

If you are struggling with loving yourself, no matter what the reason or story behind it, this next exercise is a fabulous way to combat negative mind chatter.

John Kehoe wrote a book several years back called *Mind Powers.* In it he talks about the power of affirmations, but to a grander degree. *Mind Powers*, takes less than 10 minutes per day and is about constantly affirming something to yourself until you truly feel it, believe it and live it.

Remember back in elementary school when you were learning things like 2+2=4. Well, if you were to ask a dozen strangers on the street what two plus two equals all of them would have the same answer. Why? Because it is our collective belief that 2+2=4. There is no question or doubt about it. And, how did you originally know this equation to be true? Simple – memorization. First you memorized it, then it was reinforced through your schoolwork. Possibly through counting apples or giraffes, the equation was demonstrated for you. You now knew what 2+2=4 looked like. Yet, your first knowledge of the equation began with mind powers.

In life, you may have self-doubt while others proclaim you to be kind, generous, beautiful, or smart. You may even be given examples of praise after helping someone out. For example: "Thanks so much for how kind you were to help me the other day. Your generosity is so appreciated." Yet, you still beat yourself up, saying things to yourself like "It was nothing," or "No I am not," or diminishing the compliment by telling yourself that you're not kind, generous, beautiful, smart or otherwise enough.

It's time to stop all of that. First of all, if someone sees something wonderful in you and praises you, let the compliment sink in. Accept it. Then simply say, "Thank you." When you try to push a compliment away, you do a disservice to the giver.

Whether it's a compliment or a criticism, it doesn't actually matter what others think. When they compliment or criticize you it says more about them than it does about you anyway. It is simply their opinion from their perspective, at a given moment in time.

By the way, even though I know this, I am human too. Like everyone, it's much nicer to hear compliments than criticisms. It takes effort to shrug-off insults and that is what this key is all about. Here is something to think about: it is just as important to shrug off compliments. What other people think about you isn't nearly as important as what you think about yourself. If you feel good about yourself – you'll still feel good about yourself. On the other hand – if you feel bad about yourself and someone compliments you, you're still going to feel bad about yourself. Loving yourself is like giving yourself a self-esteem inoculation. You become immune to "the good opinions of others."

The important thing is for you to feel good about your efforts, not whether someone else acknowledges it.

That's why it's imperative that you not only stand strong in how you feel or believe something about yourself, but know it to be true for yourself, Then it won't matter anymore because knowing is like armor. Nobody can penetrate it.

> "I will not be concerned at other men's not knowing me; I will be concerned at my own want of ability."
> Confucius

For example: I know I am a great father. There is absolutely no doubt in my mind and I take great pride in the fact that I love my family. So, if someone were to attempt to challenge that fact by saying something stupid like, "You suck as a father," I'd laugh. The statement would have no effect on me because I know it to be false.

That being said, I (like everyone) have an Achilles' heel. In my life there are areas I am not completely confident (no, I am not telling you what they are). What I do know is I am capable of learning and growing. I am always open to being coached in increasing my confidence and to learn how I can do things better.

Affirmation Exercise

Here is a fast and easy way for you to strengthen your confidence in a given area.

Spend five concentrated minutes every morning reciting the same affirmation of your choice. Spend another five minutes doing the same thing right before you go to bed.

For example: Three small words that say a lot. You can say, "I am worthy." Whew! This one may be hard for you. But it sure is POWERFUL. Look in the mirror when you say it. It may even bring a tear to your eye.

For the year 2011, my consistent *Mind Powers* affirmation was – 'All things are working in my favor.' No matter what the situation, I inserted my *Mind Powers* affirmation. It elevated the celebration during a great win and brightened the heaviness of any situation that attempted to bring me down. Just by saying it, I reinforced its power. It's like the saying goes... 'Believing is seeing'.

Have Gratitude–for or all the good things and all of the challenges you have experienced thus far.

In the previous key I mentioned my affirmation, 'All things are working in my favor.' It's an easy mantra when things are going well, but it is during the most trying of times that I focus on this affirmation with the most gratitude. You simply never know how the challenges in front of you are serving you, but they always are.

> "Gratitude makes sense of our past, brings peace for today, and creates a vision for tomorrow."
>
> Melody Beattie

A Moment of Gratitude

My friend's brother, Bill, has always taken great pride in his work as a dedicated employee with the Port Authority of New York. He'd been working there since he was 20 years old. It's all he's known and he loves it.

Following in his father's footsteps, Bill plans to become fully vested in his pension and then keep on working. Rather than retire, he plans to keep on working until they force him to go.

In fact, he loves it so much that when he was asked to become the spokesperson for his division during union contract negotiations back in 2001, he gladly accepted. The position required him to be away long hours after work for several weeks, if not months, attempting to influence the 'powers that be' to improve (or maintain) specific benefits and compensation for his guys. It put a huge strain on him and his family.

After a long week of negotiations, Bill left work exhausted. As he headed home for the weekend, he got a message to prepare for even longer days the following week. Contract talks had failed. Union workers were scheduled to be in front of the World Trade Center the following week handing out flyers in support of their contract negotiations. The threat of a workers' strike was imminent. An emergency meeting was scheduled for Tuesday morning to prepare for the possibility of a major shutdown of all projects throughout the city.

But on Monday night Bill received a phone call. Everything was being put on hold and Bill was to skip coming into the city and report to JFK Airport. However, there were still some permits that needed to be filed at the World Trade Center. Bill was all set to go, but his co-worker Richie assured him that he could take care of the filing.

On the morning of September 11, 2001 Bill showed up at the airport knowing Richie was at the World Trade Center dropping off the necessary paperwork.

About an hour into his work, Bill looked up to see a huge billowing black cloud blanketing the sky beyond the runway. He and his co-workers ran inside and turned the television on as the second plane crashed into the tower. He gasped as his mind raced and he grabbed his cell phone to call, only to find out he had no phone service. Frantically he attempted again and again and again before the message came over the walkie-talkie that all landline and cell service was down as a presumed terrorist attack was underway.

Staring at the unfolding chaos miles away, Bill and the entire team at JFK were instructed to stay put. There was nothing Bill could do. His heart pounded in his chest as he thought about his friend smack in the center of what would be forever known as Ground Zero. Bill was powerless as he watched the devastation unfold. Six hours later Bill finally found his friend.

As it turns out, Richie was running late the morning of 9/11. He decided to take the mid-town tunnel, hoping the extra toll would mean less traffic going into the city. It was 8:40 a.m. when he entered the tunnel. He needed to get the paperwork downtown by 9:00 a.m. Halfway through the tunnel, traffic came to a halt. He was pissed. He wished he'd taken his regular route. What the heck was the point of going this way, just to sit in traffic? There was no way he was going to make it on time. And now he was so deep in the tunnel, he couldn't even listen to the radio or use his cell phone to call and give Bill the heads up.

Richie checked his dashboard clock for the millionth time, staring as the numbers changed from minute to minute. He'd been sitting in the tunnel for almost fifteen minutes, but it seemed like a lifetime. He watched as the clock struck 8:59, 9:00, 9:01, 9:02. At 9:03 people started jumping out of their cars. One person ran up to Richie's car screaming. Then all hell broke loose as the message spread regarding the ensuing catastrophe above ground. Richie was frozen for a moment, struck by the understanding of how close he was to being there. Then he began thinking of all the others.

For the next several weeks both men worked double and triple shifts, assisting to pull bodies from the wreckage. When they were off the clock, they remained working – volunteering their time to continue.

For both of these men, gratitude is not a big enough word for the changes in schedules and traffic challenges they faced in the early morning of 9/11. As they worked together, under the rubble, tirelessly digging beneath a toxic surface, to be of service to the families who lost loved ones; these men stood together in gratitude for having had situations in their path that allowed them to continue to go home at night to be with theirs.

What happened on September 11th affected an entire nation, if not the world. Ten years later the families of the victims came together – not in mourning, but in honoring and in moving forward as the memorial in honor of those who lost their lives was finally opened.

It is not necessary to experience such a tragedy for you to sit and be grateful for the crap happening in your life. When there is crap, there is clean up, and with clean up, comes cleansing and an opportunity for a fresh start.

You must first change your perspective. Choose to stop whining and complaining. Stop being a victim. It stalls any progress and growth. Instead, search every situation for the way it can serve you. It may not be easy and sometimes it will come up simply as a learning experience. No matter what comes your way, focus on implementing The 5 Keys to Happiness. They are the foundation for *Turning Terrible into Terrific*. Once you've grasped them, you can focus on taking positive action to move forward and create the life you really want.

> "True happiness lies within"
> (I think I heard David Caradine say that on an old episode of *Kung Fu*).

Don't just read The 5 Keys to Happiness–
live them.
Don't wait for tragedy to make positive
change in your life.

What Do You REALLY Want?

Seems like a pretty simple question. There are thousands of self-help books out there written to help you get what you want. You want a new house, there's a book for that. You want a better relationship, there's a book for that. You want more money, there's a book for that too.

In fact, if you can think of something you want, I can pretty much guarantee that somewhere someone (or more likely thousands of some ones) has written a book about it.

Thousands of books? Yes. Thousands. So, why keep reading this one? The answer is simple; because those other books miss the most important question.

I'm not saying there isn't a lot of relevant, even great information found in them. However, it seems to me they don't offer long-lasting change because they simply don't ask (or answer) the proper question. Asking, "How do I get what I want?" is the wrong question.

See, I don't care about what you want. Frankly, neither should you. Think about it. What you *want* is often driven by whim and subject to change at any moment. I care about asking and assisting you in figuring out the answer to a deeper, more important question:

"What do you REALLY want?"

Allow me to illustrate. You pull up to the drive-thru window of your favorite burger joint with a yearning for a cheeseburger and shake. After placing your order you ask, "Oh, may I add something? I think I want fries with that." The aspiring burgermeister explains how sorry he is, but they are out of fries. You think for a second, shrug your shoulders, and order the onion rings instead.

Hmmm. Interesting. Why didn't you freak out? Why didn't you demand to see the owner and insist that your entire order be cancelled? Or tell the young burger guy where he or she could shove it? Most likely it's because missing fries simply wasn't a big deal and it wasn't a big deal because you may have wanted fries, but you didn't REALLY want them. What you REALLY wanted was the best darn burger you've ever come across and the greatest tasting shake in all of history. Meanwhile, you simply settled on the onion rings because they were something greasy to go with the meal.

Now let's say you did make a big-ass stink about the fries. You got all mad at the poor young guy who managed to stay quite calm during your rant, didn't charge you for the onion rings and gave you a coupon for free fries on your next visit. You then proceeded to sit in the parking lot with a huge sourpuss while eating the burger and shake that didn't taste nearly as fabulous as you had envisioned beforehand, because you were too busy sulking over a secondary item that wasn't the focus of your visit.

For most people, this is exactly how they go about everything in their lives. They either settle for things they don't REALLY want or while making a big stink over the less important things in their lives, they miss the joy from the things they REALLY do want.

Because they are never truly impassioned by anything, they are unwilling to stick it out when things don't go their way or whine about it afterwards. They often push what they really want aside in search of something simpler to fill the void they can't seem to satisfy. They settle for less than they asked for. They get onion rings instead of the fries. They spend so much time half-heartedly chasing the things they want, or more likely the things that society has told them they should want, that they slowly allow compromise after compromise after compromise until they reduce their existence to a level of comfortably miserable – never having achieved what they really wanted.

Here is my advice: Stop chasing what you want and start focusing on what you REALLY want.

Have you ever noticed that the more you truly want something, the more likely you are to achieve it? Can you remember a time when you wanted something so badly you were willing to do whatever it took to get it? Do you remember how you felt when you achieved it? It felt great, admit it!

When you REALLY want something, you'll be willing to make the sacrifices necessary in order to reach your goal.

So what do you REALLY want?

That simple question could take you a lifetime to figure out or it could happen in an instant. In fact, these last few paragraphs may have led you to the realization that you've been on the wrong path to happiness. If that is the case, then it's time to stop filling your days with busy trivial work that is slowly, but inevitably, eroding your spirit. It's time to change direction, figure out what you REALLY want and go for it!

> "Make what you (REALLY) want, non-negotiable and make the problem intolerable.... Don't do the best you can, do what-ever it takes."
>
> Keith Cunningham

If you are one of those people who think you've already achieved *all* that you REALLY wanted. You are ready to reach for something more. How do I know? Because you wouldn't be reading this if you were content with things exactly as they are. My question to you is simple, "What do you REALLY want next?"

For most of you, the one thing you REALLY want remains outside your grasp. For some, it's still vague or unclear. For even more you are saying, "But Dennis, there is more than one thing I REALLY want." For those of you with that statement in your head, the answer is simple – focus on one 'want' at a time. Otherwise your energy gets stretched too thin and your mind can't decide which direction to go. It's like the law of diminishing returns. In simple terms: you do more and more, but get nothing <u>done</u>.

> "Enlightenment must come little by little - otherwise it would overwhelm."
>
> Idries Shah

Once you've managed to achieve one of your "REALLY want" goals, you can master the technique of managing several REALLY wants at the same time. In the meantime, let's focus on the K.I.S.S. principle (keep it simple silly).

> "Consider the postage stamp; its usefulness consists in the ability to stick to one thing until it gets there."
>
> Josh Billings

<u>Clarity = Power</u>

It is vital to get clear on what you REALLY want in order to map out a plan to attain it. Otherwise, it's like driving to a town you've never been without having a map or directions. Ah, some of you are familiar with that. I can hear your spouses giggling in the background. I can see the guilty smirk on your face as you lower your head, caught. Yup. You're the one that decided to take the amazing short-cut that lasted three extra hours because you didn't want to ask for help or admit you missed the turn-off 60 miles back. I know you. In fact, I have been you (I am so grateful for my GPS right now).

See, without clear direction you (and your passengers) are powerless over how you will reach your desired destination. It doesn't mean you won't get there, but if the route is not plotted out, the journey will be a lot longer and more painful. Why make your life more difficult than it needs to be?

"But Dennis, how do I find clarity?" Excellent question.

Although not necessarily easy, it is important to be *very* specific when visualizing what you REALLY want. In the last chapter I gave you an exercise to assist you with loving the things you have right now. I asked you to write 100 things you have right now. In that case, you were listing tangible items, maybe some feelings, emotions, and experiences. You were probably able to write several items easily and quickly. Maybe even a lot of things. Then it got harder and harder. I am sure some of you didn't even bother to finish. If you did – you got to the juice. You got to the deeper, more specific, details of what you love right now. You may have even had a few breakthroughs. Good for you. That was the point of the exercise.

This next exercise is similar to the one in the previous chapter. For those who did not complete the previous exercises my question to you is: why are you investing time in reading this book but not making the effort to do the work?

My suggestion from this point forward is to make a conscious effort to be committed to the process. Otherwise, you will not get the results you desire. I also strongly suggest you take the time to go back and do the previous exercises at some point in order to gain the maximum benefit this book has to offer.

My goal is for you to have FUN. That is why I've written it all in a very casual style, yet I am also here to push your buttons and get you to get a bit uncomfortable, to stretch your comfort zone. I do this because, in my experience, people typically only change when it is too painful not to.

The aim is for you to turn terrible into terrific. Finding out what you REALLY want plays a huge part in that; and commitment is crucial in understanding how to get where you say you REALLY want to go. There is a fabulous quote by Zen Master Cherie Huber "How you do anything, is how you do everything." So STOP screwing around and do the work. *That* is how you get results.

Okay, enough of my rant. For all of you who have been diligently participating, the previous little sidebar should not have affected you in any manner (except for the few moments of extra reading). Take it as a lesson for those times you don't feel like doing the work.

To those for whom my rant resonated - I commend you for reading this line and continuing, because it means you weren't stopped by a little verbal ass-whoopin'. For the rest... well, they're not actually reading anymore so it REALLY doesn't matter, does it? 'Cause what *I* REALLY want is to assist those who are committed to making positive change actually achieve what they REALLY want.

Clarity Exercise

The following exercise is a very powerful visualization technique that will assist you in finding clarity in what you REALLY want. For this exercise you will need your journal or notebook again. You will also need a pen. No pencils please. This exercise must be done in one sitting. It will take anywhere from 20 minutes to half an hour. Make sure to set aside the proper time to complete it.

1) <u>On the cover of your notebook or journal write:</u> *Reality Journal.*

I like the term Reality Journal because it's what you are looking to manifest. Dreams are wonderful, but even by definition they relate to intangible thoughts and desires. Our aim is to manifest REAL results - things that have actual, physical existence.

In the previous chapter you used this journal during some appreciation exercises. See, your Reality Journal works!

2) <u>On the inside cover write:</u> *This or something better: All things are working in my favor.*

Why? Because it sounds good, don't you think? Actually, there are two reasons. First, it will assist you in remaining flexible. Clarity is vital, so is flexibility, and the first part, "this or something better", allows for even greater possibilities than you can imagine. The second half, "all things are working in my favor," goes back to my description of *Mind Powers* earlier in the book. Working that muscle of belief with certainty, this phrase (especially if stated aloud each day) will assist you in solidifying your belief in what you REALLY want while remaining unattached to how and when things materialize. All you have to focus on is taking positive action toward your goal.

3) <u>At the top of the first page, title your list.</u>

The title of your list is the outcome of what you REALLY want. In other words, if you are looking for a new career and you're not sure where to begin - this is your starting point. Therefore, your title might look like this:

Example: *The Career of My REALITY*

If you are looking for a career in a specific field, then go one step further:

Example: *The Nursing Career of My REALITY*

4) <u>Using every other line on the page, write down all the attributes of what you REALLY want.</u>

Don't hold back. This means every minute detail relating to what you REALLY want. What does it look like? What does it feel like? What are your surroundings? Who are the people you are involved? Etc., etc., etc.

Example:
The Nursing Career of My REALITY

My nursing career involves working in a hospital.

I am surrounded by incredible co-workers in my nursing career.

I wake up looking forward to going to work everyday.

I am challenged everyday at work.

I love my career.

I am involved with helping children in my nursing career.

I get paid very well (feel free to put a $ figure) for the work I do.

I have an incredible 90-day evaluation.

I receive continual pay raises in my nursing career.

I am respected in my nursing career.

My nursing career is incredibly rewarding.

When you get stuck... keep going. This is where the juice is! This is where your list becomes your vision. While you are doing this it's very important to not look back and review. Simply keep on writing.

Yes, you will get stuck. It's natural. Getting stuck is a good thing. It reflects one of two things: your mind is attempting to take you out or this isn't what you REALLY want. Either way – it's PERFECT. My guess is, if you've gotten this far in the process, most likely if you feel stuck – it's your mind attempting to take you out.

Fight back!

How do you do that? Simple... keep going. See the brilliance in this exercise – in the beginning it's simply a list – a list of wants, desires, or pre-conceived thoughts. Once you get past the sticky point, you are now **envisioning** what it is you REALLY want. As you keep writing, your vision will become more and more **clear**, therefore, more **powerful**.

Okay, now is the time to stop reading and do the exercise. Go ahead. I am not going anywhere. I'll be right here when you are done.

* * *

Cool, huh? I bet you feel pretty empowered right now. Excellent!

5) <u>Now, let go and let the list Be.</u>

Close the notebook and let the magic begin. This last step will be the most challenging for you, but it's one of the most critical. STOP obsessing. You wrote the list. You did the work. Now let the list work for you. Remember: Clarity = Power. You are probably clearer about what you REALLY want right now than you have ever been before.

Anytime you feel doubt, pick up the book, open it and begin reading your list. It will quickly remind you what it is you REALLY want, especially when you are presented with something that doesn't feel quite right.

It is important to remember that you skipped every other line for a reason. It's called flexibility. Not compromise, but flexibility. When you are presented with an opportunity that feels great, sounds great, and looks great – take a look at your list. You'll know even before you look.

If everything feels, sounds and looks great... I'll bet almost all (if not all) of the criteria you wrote down have been met. For those items that haven't quite been met – that is what the 'in-between' lines (blank lines between your criteria) allow for, a slight change of heart or a means of letting go - because those points were not the most vital for you to find your happiness. This 'space' also allows room for you to grow.

Take Action

That's right; you are not quite done with this chapter. You've come so far. Don't give up now. This one is not nearly as involved as the last one, but it is equally as important.

Now that you are clear, empowered, and feeling great about what it is you REALLY want, you can make your list into reality with positive action in the direction of that goal.

> "If one advances confidently in the direction of his dreams and endeavors to live the life, which he has imagined, he will meet with a success unexpected in common hours."
>
> Henry David Thoreau

Action Exercise

In the same journal, leave a few clean sheets of paper between your previous reality list (call it breathing room...) and this next exercise.

On a clean sheet of paper write the words 'Brain Storming' at the top. Now make a list of steps you can take to achieve what you REALLY want. The list does not have to be in any particular order or any specific length. Think about the big things that will need to be done as well as the smallest of things. All are equally important at this point.

Start... now!

(If you are reading this, you are not doing the exercise. Get going!)

Seriously, your pen should be moving a mile a minute. Don't wait to do this. Until you write measurable and attainable tasks, what you say you REALLY want is just a dream.

Don't just do it, be happy doing it!

* * *

Done? See, that didn't hurt very much, did it?

Now pick one thing that you can accomplish today. Yes, today.

Who cares if it's nighttime and you've stayed up late enough as it is doing the past several exercises, too bad. There has got to be *something* on that list you can do right now to ensure a great start for tomorrow. It may simply be making the declaration (promise to yourself) to wake up a half hour earlier and accomplish one of the tasks you've just written down. But don't just declare it; set your alarm to get up half an hour early.

Next step – complete the task by actually getting your butt out of bed, turning on the computer for example, and doing the job you promised yourself you would accomplish.

> "Being the richest man in the cemetery doesn't matter to me. Going to bed at night saying we've done something wonderful, that's what matters to me."
>
> Steve Jobs

Decide what you REALLY want.
Commit to one thing at a time.
There is power in writing lists.
Do the work.

I Had a Plan

Since getting my first credit card at 18, I was diligent at paying off my balance every month. But after graduating college and struggling in the job market, from 2008 to 2010, I'd become entirely dependent on my credit cards. In fact, as my balances climbed, I also found myself dependent on my father's credit cards, just to get by. I used my father's credit cards to pay off the recurring minimum payments on my own cards. It was terrible. When I'd find a job, I would try to pay him back and pay my cards down. But, I was inconsistent and I was struggling.

Financially, that period does not hold a lot of pride for me; in fact I used to feel very ashamed. I'd done a lot of self-development work and been working on my emotional and spiritual growth for a long time. I'd found joy and peace in my life, but I knew I was missing a vital component in my happiness – confidence. Looking at the reality of my debt was not something I thought I would be doing at 29. I'd lost confidence in the possibility that I could actually change my financial situation.

That self-awareness forced me to take inventory in all areas of my life and ask myself where I needed and wanted to make changes. With a little help from an acquaintance, I began to seriously look at setting financial and life goals. Number one on my list was to pay off my debt.

My original plan was to pay off both my student loans and my credit card debt within one year. Once I calculated the amount of money it would take to do that compared to the reality of my income at that moment, I changed my plan to focus solely on my credit card debt. I created a strong foundation for myself. I changed my money habits so I could live my life while I learned to be okay with my debt. I realized it represented both education and necessity at a time in my life when I did not understand how to manage my money. It was up to me to stop it from defining my future.

I stuck to my plan like glue for the first few months. I was rigid because I wanted to get it. I did not want to repeat my old patterns anymore. However, I realized since my income was not constant, there were going to be times when I could not pay as much as I had planned to pay. However, I never missed a payment – even if it was just the minimum. Once work started up again I was back at it in full force.

The day I made my final payment, one year and four months later, the sense of relief, accomplishment and confidence was more than words could express. I had turned what I had once detested into a success!

I learned many things from that experience and I continue to apply the same principles in all areas of my life. First, I am committed to the end result and I am open to the journey to get there. I am also aware there may be times to let go or adjust. Secondly, I realize making change does not have to be difficult and it certainly won't kill me. I do not have to sacrifice to get there. I just have to look at the challenge and decide whether it will stop me or simply slow me down until I gather the resources (physical, mental, emotional and spiritual) to move beyond it. And finally, I have a new perspective on the amount of energy it will take to tackle my next goal - my student loans. In fact, I am already there. I can confidently say, 'This is totally doable!'

Kelly M.
Ontario, Canada

A Fork in the Road

We've already established there are the things you want and then there are the things you REALLY want. Why is it so important to know what you REALLY want? Because if you don't REALLY want it, you're more likely to give up when the going gets too tough.

There is another reason why it's so imperative to know what you REALLY want. If you don't know what you REALLY want, you might just get what you *want*, only to realize that what you got wasn't what you REALLY wanted after all. And you did all the work to get it. Well, doesn't that suck?

I know that last paragraph can be a little confusing so let me offer another tool you can use to evaluate your level of *want*. On a scale of 1-10, rate the things you want between 4 and 8. The higher the number, the greater the desire, and more chance you'll put forth some effort into the result. The things you REALLY want would rate 9 or 10. These are the things you feel compelled to do. You have a need to attain these goals for deeper reasons than simply (now listen for the slight whine in my voice), "because I want to," (which any six-year-old can say). What you REALLY want is not driven by whim, but by purpose.

If you find yourself asking, "What about the things I want that sit right there, right on the cusp. Those things I rate a solid 8, but not quite a 9?"

Nope. Not good enough. Take whatever it is off the REALLY want list. Until you are certain whatever you are yearning for ranks at least a 9, don't bother reaching for it, 'cause you don't REALLY want it and when the going gets tough... the 8.5 gets goin'. In other words – you'll give up!

> "Life isn't worth living unless you're willing to take some big chances and go for broke."
>
> Eliot Wiggington

What? You don't have anything that ranks that high? Well, then you definitely need to keep on reading because *Turning Terrible into Terrific* needs to be your goal. You can't get to terrific if you don't see anything in life (including what you want to reach for) worthy of a 10.

But, I want more than....

On the other hand, you may have a whole list of 9's and 10's. That's great, but it's not about the quantity of things you REALLY want. It's about knowing how to prioritize your REALLY wants so you may achieve all that you desire.

In life, we often experience conflicting desires. We aspire to have more in our lives, whether it's financial prosperity, better relationships, or deeper spirituality. We want more than one thing. That's just normal for humans. However, sometimes one thing comes at the expense of another. For example: you want 'A' and you also REALLY want 'B'.

Sometimes the path to 'A' and 'B' lie along the same road. You travel right through 'A' (what you want) on your way to 'B' (what you REALLY want). Hopefully, when this happens you get to enjoy a little of 'A' as you mosey along toward what you REALLY want – 'B'. In other words, don't get too comfortable along the road and allow 'A' to distract you from your goal (which is B). Don't lose your momentum and yearning to reach for 'B'. If you stop at 'A' and don't continue (which many people do), you've settled. You may even feel pretty comfortable. Guess what? Comfortable can be terrible, especially in the land of mediocrity.

Career goals are a prime example of this. Suppose you are aiming for a promotion. You are up against five other people vying for the same position and unfortunately after a long arduous process, you don't get the job. You are, however, assured an identical position will be coming up in less than six weeks allowing you a second attempt in attaining what you really want which, also happens to be why you came to the company in the first place.

Meanwhile, one of the managers who interviewed you sees your talent (of course) and offers you a similar, but lesser monetary promotion, in a different division and using a different skill set. The job is yours, should you accept it. The only clincher is that the manager has asked for you to commit to staying in the position for at least 18 months in order to ensure stability within the scope of the offer.

You are faced with a decision: *A Fork in the Road.* Do you take the lesser promotion?

You would? Really? Even if it means a change in the trajectory of your career goal? I get it. Your reasoning is that it will only affect you in the short-term. Hmmm. Interesting. It's amazing how many people I've met who have taken a job they didn't actually like or weren't passionate about only to find themselves still doing it after 18 years.

Oh. Now you've changed your tune. You are thinking it's better to hold out for the next six weeks so you can take a second shot at competing for the position you really want?

Good for you. However, before you make the final decision, I've got something to add to the equation. Along with the uncertainty of attaining the job you claim to really want, if you wait, the opportunity for the lesser offer will be long gone. Now what do you do?

You choose.

> "Make the decision, make it with confidence, and the world will be yours."
>
> Jaren L. Davis

In life, faster and easier paths to success do not always lead you to what you really want and to what you truly desire. Often, the faster and easier path actually leads you away from what you really want.

When this happens, your temporary success only serves to keep you in a state of lack, it keeps you wanting something else, and it keeps you comfortably miserable.

In order to stay on the right path it is essential that you are crystal clear about what it is that you really want, why you want it, and what you would be willing to do to have it.

Sometimes the fastest way over the wall of success is to use a ladder. Just make sure the ladder is leaning against the right wall.

> "We gain strength, and courage, and confidence by each experience in which we really stop to look fear in the face... We must do that which we think we cannot."
>
> Eleanor Roosevelt

Clarity is Power.
If you get clear on what you REALLY
want, you'll know what to do at the fork
in the road.

Know Your "Why"

Turning Terrible into Terrific is a decision, a choice you make in an instant. However, maintaining *Terrific* takes clarity, consistency, determination, and of course – practice.

Have you ever taken one of those long tests to see what kind of leader you are or what type of career you should pursue? A personality test perhaps? Did you ever notice in the 10,000 questions they ask in any of those types of tests, there were actually only about 20 questions – asked a thousand times, only with slight changes in wording or perspective? I am sure by now you've noticed there have been some repetitive themes running through each chapter so far. In order to truly change your thoughts, you must be persistent in creating new strategies to do so.

By now you may have actually taken some action, possibly even come across a fork in the road. Maybe you are wondering which way to go, or have decided on a direction, but now you're questioning your decision. Perfect.

I've got a vital piece of the puzzle for you. In order to keep momentum and remain steadfast in achieving what you really want, you must also know your *Why*.

I can hear you now, "What the heck does that mean?"

Simply, your *Why* is your propelling force. The thing that makes you keep on going when you are faced with indecision, fear, or trepidation. Ask yourself, "Why do I want what I want?"

Not sure. That's okay. Here is a list of more specific questions that will help you. Ask yourself: *Why* do I want this? *Why* is it important? *Why* is it worth it? *Why* am I compelled to do it? How will my life, relationships, finances be different when I achieve what I REALLY want?

If you cannot answer these questions then it's likely you don't really want whatever it is you say you are aiming for. If you are reaching for a goal and you have no substance behind it, it's going to be a lot harder to achieve it. It's worse than attempting to drive to a place you've never been before without directions. You also have no gas!

In the very beginning of this book, I explained my *Why* for writing it. Remember? I opened up and admitted that I am among the more than 200 million people who wish to be published, I confessed how this book acts as a platform for future speaking engagements and workshops, and explained how I want to make a difference in peoples' lives. I was very clear, concise, and forthcoming. I know my *Why*.

Need another example? Okay.

Let's say Jim has decided he really wants to be a millionaire. He wants a net worth of $5,000,000. He doesn't know how he's going to do it, but he really wants it. He says he's willing to do whatever it takes. Giving him a map of step-by-step instructions on what it will take for him to achieve this is actually the easy part. The big question to pose to Jim would be, why? Why does he want $5,000,000? Why does he want to be a millionaire? Most likely the answer lies somewhere in his 100-list. Somewhere in that list lies the reason behind what this goal means to him—what it would allow him to do—what it would provide. Most likely he doesn't have to look back at his list. He knows it already. The meaning sits on the surface, but in order to achieve this lofty goal, it is imperative that Jim be conscious of it and uses it as a beacon to his success when success seems far away. In fact, if he delves into his *Why,* he may not actually need, nor REALLY want to be a multi-millionaire at all.

Know your *Why.*

> "People are not lazy. They simply have impotent goals - that is, goals that do not inspire them."
>
> Tony Robbins

Knowing your why can be useful in eliminating activities that don't get you what you really want, supporting the idea of 'working smarter not harder'.

Not sure of what your *Why* is, but feel you know what you REALLY want? Turn back to the "What do you REALLY Want" chapter and read the example: The Nursing Career of my Reality.

Can you see this person's *Why*?

Sure you can. Why does she want the nursing career of her reality? So she can feel good about what she does for a living. So she can help ill children, afford the lifestyle that she chooses, and continue to grow her income. These are most likely her propelling forces, and there are others that we do not see as her 100-list is not complete.

When you re-read your 100-list notice any common themes, those are your whys (yes, you may find you have more than one).

> "He who has a why to live can bear almost any how."
> Friedrich Nietzsch|

The stronger the why, the harder you'll work for what you want, hence the reason you wrote 100 items. Anything less and you may have a false why. Your *Why* is sometimes hidden. The first 25-50 items on the list may simply be surface reasons. If you truly took the time to do the exercise, you saw and possibly felt the difference and if you didn't finish the list at all... well doesn't that speak volumes? Once again remember, how you do anything is how you do everything. You bought a book on *Turning Terrible into Terrific*. Either your purchase was an investment and you are willing to do the work or it was a frivolous expenditure you hoped would contain a magic pill that would give you everything you wanted without doing the work. I didn't say it would be easy.

Actually, I do offer one magic pill and I said it earlier in the book. It's called choice. You can choose to be happy. You can choose life to be terrific (or not). That decision happens at the speed of thought. Doing the necessary work happens at the speed of life.

> "There is no passion to be found playing small - in settling for a life that is less than the one you are capable of living."
> Nelson Mandela

 No matter what the goal, you've got to know the reason you are looking to achieve it. Otherwise, when the going gets tough – you won't show up!

Be Better Than Yourself

One of the biggest causes of discontent is the perceived inability to measure up to some idealistic goal of what we are supposed to be, do, or have.

We humans share a natural tendency to want to do things better than the other guy. We struggle to 'Keep Up With The Jones'. We (and by we, I mean you) work long hours in the hope that the boss will notice we are doing more than the person in the next cubicle and that we will advance to the next position of higher paying tedium.

I want to be clear about something. Growth is good. Increasing one's knowledge is good. Striving for better relationships, greater prosperity, and spiritual enlightenment is good.

The problem occurs when you start to compare your current level of attainment or success to the level attained by those around you. Once this happens, your ability to be happy becomes dependent on you comparing yourself to others.

It seems these days we not only feel compelled to keep up with The Jones' but expect to be able to keep up with The Kardashians'.

Stop that!

> "Don't bother just to be better than your contemporaries or predecessors. Try to be better than yourself."
> William Faulkner

There is absolutely no need or reason to compare your progress with anyone else's. This is your journey, your life. Set your own benchmarks, focus and push forward to achieve them.

When you compare your own performance to others there is a high risk of either overvaluing or undervaluing your successes.

The comparisons are ridiculously unfair anyway. We all have different skills and talents. What may be very easy for someone else in one area may be incredibly difficult for someone else in that same area.

By entertaining thoughts that you are not as smart as them, or as funny as them, or as good-looking as them, or as rich as them, keeps you in the mindset of 'not being enough' and completely invalidates the fact that you worked your butt off for your achievements.

Here is a tip: Always dream and shoot higher than you know you can and commit 100% to the achievement of your goals. You'll be surprised just how much you can accomplish.

Here's another tip: Be okay with where you are along the way and the amount of time it may take to get there. Be okay with the fears and excitements you may encounter along the way. It's part of the journey.

People don't get on a roller coaster anticipating the moment when the cars screech to a halt at the end lamenting the fact that it took long and that it was a hard climb in the beginning and that the ride was filled with dips and bumps and unexpected twists and turns. They get on the roller coaster for the thrills and chill of the ride. They revel in the excitement of the unexpected and relish the unexpected twists and turns, and when the ride is over, they want to go again.

Life is a roller coaster....Enjoy the ride!

> "Shoot for the moon. If you miss you will still be among the stars."
>
> Les Brown

Acknowledge Your Successes

Okay. Now you know not to compare your performance to the performance of others. Another powerful tool in *Turning Terrible into Terrific* is to make sure to acknowledge your successes along the way.

When we acknowledge our successes, big and small, it provides power to persevere.

So many people focus on the negative, or what went wrong, when reviewing their own or others' performances. Yes, I know you are judging. It's almost built into our society. Magazines, TV shows (especially reality TV), and sports are inundated with judgment first.

Magazines find fault with stars, TV shows blast all that went wrong in people's cooking, dance routine, even dating style, and sports' fans scream obscenities from high in the stands when a team or player they supposedly admire makes an error.

When it comes to your own performance the better tack (tactic?) is one of acknowledging successes first. In fact, in order to be better, it is absolutely imperative.

Why? Because if you start with all that went wrong first it's like throwing yourself into quicksand of failure. With each harsh criticism of yourself you go deeper and deeper until you can barely breathe. You have to struggle just to keep your head above the gloppy mess that is pulling you down, faster and faster, leaving no room to recognize anything that went well for you. You're stuck so far down in the crap you can't recognize anything you did well, you are simply struggling to survive.

Stop doing that!

When evaluating your performance, you've already learned not to compare yourself to others. Secondly, make sure you evaluate yourself in a constructive manner.

Here is what that looks like.

Evaluation Questions

1) What was Terrific? In other words, what went well?

2) What was terrible? In other words, what didn't go well?

3) How can you make changes in order to turn terrible into terrific? What can you do different next time to improve the outcome?

When evaluating your performance always begin with what you did well. Again, I can hear you now (in that whining voice of yours), "But Dennis you don't understand it was the worst speech I've ever given. I totally screwed it up.... blah, blah, blah."

Turn off that annoyingly negative voice in your head and listen (okay – read).

I'll ask again, "What was truly terrific?" They don't have to be huge triumphs, but simply positive things that you were responsible for in the midst of all else that occurred in a given circumstance. I strongly suggest you write them down. Yes, another list.   Writing them down will make them have more impact for you.   Plus, by writing your triumphs down you will have a record of your improvement. Growth often occurs gradually. Sometimes when things change slowly, we don't even realize that they have changed at all. It's like the mark on the wall that your mom drew of your height each year. You didn't feel that you grew taller each day but those lines inside the closet showed that you grew four inches that year. Recording all of the positive things you have accomplished will serve to counteract your negative self-talk when things don't quite go the way you had hoped. That is why it is critical to look for the positive in any situation.

For example, let's say you did give the worst speech ever. Instead of whining about your performance and bashing yourself unmercifully, you realize there were some really great things that came out of your performance. When you took the time to evaluate your performance as a whole, you remember being commended for your knowledge on the subject and recall the hours of research you managed to do even with a jam-packed schedule. You also arrived early to the event, which led you to meeting a person you'd been attempting to get an appointment with for months. Additionally, you had all your notes completely prepared, you smiled, and you had a great set of opening, engaging questions. Oh, and don't forget you also remembered to thank the person who invited you, had a super conversation with the head of the organization, and you were asked back in the spring. Best of all – you remembered to zip up the fly on your trousers this time.

Hmmm...not so bad after all.

> "Life will give you whatever experience is most helpful for the evolution of your consciousness."
>
> Eckhart Tolle

When you know things didn't go the way you planned, write anything and everything that went well down on paper or voice it, and I mean – everything. You remembered to go to the bathroom beforehand, you remembered your water, your suit was pressed to perfection, you remembered to get a haircut the day before (that looked great by the way), you remembered to put deodorant on (hey... this one is very important, especially in situations that can be nerve-wracking). Every detail counts – event the smallest ones. (Especially the zipping of the fly; I learned that one the hard way.)

Okay, so those are the things that worked. See, if you were feeling bad about your performance, I bet you feel a bit better now.

You are ready to face what didn't work with strength, power, and objectivity.

Move on to what was terrible. This doesn't mean you beat yourself up. It means you make an honest evaluation of what things didn't go the way you had hoped.

Maybe the projector stopped working and threw off your timing. It took a while to get back on track and grounded. Maybe you were called-out by a listener for not knowing the answer to a question or maybe you lost control of the audience for a moment because you forgot to set a tight context for the workshop. Maybe you felt rushed after messing up and forgot a full portion of your presentation. (by the way... you are the only one that noticed). Maybe you wanted to thank a specific individual and forgot.

Okay, so you messed up. Move onto the next question.

How can you turn this around next time?

See, you're not deep in the sludge. You may not be feeling fabulous. It may have taken some creativity to find something terrific in the situation, but you see the big picture and how things can go better the next time because you started from a positive, proactive approach of evaluating the event as a whole. Now you can make adjustments or implement changes to ensure things go better next time.

For example: You may want to test the projector before the audience arrives, find some techniques that help you keep your composure when things go wrong, write a list of those individuals you wish to thank so you don't forget and have a system for your notes that allows you to ensure you remember each page.

Even if you feel it was the worst performance of your entire career, if someone congratulates you – say thank you and shut up! Do not go into your 'story' with them.

What they saw was a polished professional presentation. Could you have done it better? Listen carefully to this answer... No, you could not have. This may be difficult to grasp, but you did the best you could have done based on that particular day, with that particular audience, and that particular projector, and you particular level of experience with that particular presentation at that particular time. It could not have been any different. Can it be different next time? Of course it can, and it should, because you will have grown from the experience.

Most likely they didn't see it the way you did. One of the most critical elements of having a terrific life is to stop being so critical about your own performance. Look for the things that went well. Be OK with the things that could have gone better knowing that you will improve upon them the next time around.

> "Most people achieved their greatest success one step beyond what looked like their greatest failure."
>
> Brian Tracy

 Constructively evaluating your performance in a given situation is crucial to making positive change to *Turning Terrible into Terrific*.

Be Willing to Offend

Most people want everyone to like them. They settle on what they get, rather than what they want because they don't want to make a fuss or hurt anyone's feelings. You know, they order their steak rare and eat it even when it comes to the table cold and well done. They say things like "you look fabulous" when their best friend comes out of the dressing room in the most hideous dress they've ever seen, and they look the other way when a co-worker is being harassed at the office.

Wrong! Take a stand.

In order for your life to be Terrific, you must be willing to offend. This does not mean be offensive. It means you must be willing to take a stand for the things you want or believe in, without worrying about the possibility that you may ruffle some feathers. Standing your ground and owning 'who' you are gives you the ability and power to achieve your desires instead of conforming to other people's expectations of you. Standing your ground allows you to stop settling for less than you deserve. Trying to make everyone like you is simply – terrible. It's too much work and the fact is... it's a recipe for disaster.

When was the last time you met a group of two or more people that agreed on everything (or anything for that matter)? We all have different tastes, ideas, feelings toward, and opinions about – everything. Exhausting yourself in an attempt to make everyone happy or wanting to have everyone like you is – crazy. It's not even possible and sounds absolutely daunting.

> "Be yourself. Above all, let who you are, what you are, and what you believe, shine through..."
>
> John Jakes

Think about it, even Mother Teresa was not liked by everyone. In fact, many people/organizations didn't like her at all. In 1990 Germaine Greer a feminist activist declared Mother Teresa a religious imperialist. Some

Hindus in her own country spoke out against her actions of hope and help. Crazy, huh?

My point is: stand up for what you believe in and stop trying to be liked by all. Be willing to offend. Doing so will benefit you immensely, and once you are confident in what you will or will not tolerate for yourself, you will have the ability to stand up for those unable to do so for themselves and make a substantial positive difference in your world.

Greg Mooers Montana, founder of Heart Virtue Inc., is an incredible speaker and trainer who focuses on love and relationships and speaks about the importance of being the hero – the importance of unabashedly expressing your authentic self.

Be the hero.

In his talks he gives an example that stems from him witnessing a young child (approximately eight years old) being severely scolded by a parent in a grocery store. Greg was standing in line at the checkout counter when he overheard this woman screaming at her little boy.

Greg also noticed the people who passed close by her. They kept walking. Some lowered their heads.

Others whispered to each other and peered back, shaking their heads in disdain. When the woman began berating the young child again, Greg could not stand idly by any longer. He walked over, and although his hands were trembling, he stood face to face with the woman and said, "Please treat that child with respect."

She stared back at him, stunned. "This is none of your business," she frowned. Greg calmly retorted, "It's none of my business if you do this in your living room, but when I have to look over and see your little boy standing there shaking while he's holding that cereal box, it's my business. Please treat that child with respect." The woman puffed and shook her head in frustration. She threw the cereal box in the basket, took her boy's hand and ran out of the store.

Greg was shaking as much as the little boy had been. He had dealt with the mother's rage, rather than ignoring it. You may be thinking, thank goodness he stopped her from hurting that little boy any further. Or you may feel Greg crossed a line. Possibly, you are worried about what happened to the child later that night, when his mother got him outside of public eye.

No matter what you are thinking – none of it can be wrong. It comes from your own experience. However, Greg would say something to the effect of: "That's not the point. The point is what the woman was doing challenged my values. I had no choice but to defend what I believe, which is that no child deserves to be treated such a way and scarred in that manner." He'd also add how in his mind, he'd hope the woman drove home and thought about her actions and for the first time in her life realized what she was doing and how she was acting was affecting her son.

See, life is about perspective. Greg could only hope that the woman's eyes were open to her actions regarding her son and that life became easier for both her and her son in that moment.

> "Courage is what it takes to stand up and speak; courage is also what it takes to sit down and listen."
> Winston Churchill

Remember, that being 'willing to offend' does not mean being "offensive". Greg did not engage the mother in the store in order to cause her harm. His actions were to protect an endangered child.

In literature, the Hero defends what he or she

believes in and is willing to take a stand in a strong, well-intentioned way. By doing so, they improve life around them.

We all have an inner hero inside us. Unfortunately, while a person's inner Hero is often willing to come out to defend others, it cowers under a mental rock when it comes to defending themselves against the damage caused by their own subconscious.

People often inflict harm on themselves, both by the actions they choose to take, or not to take, and in the way they speak about themselves. Many have an inner voice that can really 'trash talk'. Their inner voice points out their mistakes, limitations and shortcomings. It is this unsupportive subconscious voice that largely determines the actions you will or won't take in your search for happiness.

We are our own worst critics and instead of defending ourselves against our own negative talk, we live into the internal assault on who we are and the choices we make in life.

It's amazing how we can be our own biggest bully. I call it the Bully Within. I think it's time to fight back and change that.

I once read an article about a teacher in New York who gave her class an exercise to illustrate the painful effects of bullying. She had the children take out a piece of blank paper and told them to crumple it up, stomp on it and really mess it up, but instructed them not to rip it. Then she had them unfold the paper, smooth it out and look at how scarred and dirty is was. She instructed them to apologize. To tell the paper how sorry they were for messing it up. She even had them make every attempt to remove the effects of what they'd done.

The students did as instructed, but of course the damage was done. She pointed out all the creases, grime, dirt and even some frayed tears in the paper.

She then asked the students to look at the paper and explained how no matter how hard they might try, the damage will never go away. She further explained how this was an example of the effects of what happens when a child bullies another child. The looks on the faces of the children told her that the message hit home.

I was astounded over a statistic I recently read. According to the non-profit Love Our Children USA, one-in-five children and teens in the United States have admitted to being bullied at some point. What also amazed me was how many of my adult friends and mentors said they remembered being bullied as a child.

It got me thinking. Somehow, I believe the effects of bullying are carried long after the event. Earlier, I gave examples of how some people will give up on getting what they really want, are afraid they might offend someone or lack the ability to 'Be the Hero' in a situation that merits taking a stand.

I think I've found the reason why. Whether carried over from childhood or developed as an adult, the biggest bullying happens in the six inches between the ears. It's the Bully Within that's been holding you back.

According to Dan Olweus, of the Olweus Bullying Prevention Program (theolweus.org) there are three important components of bullying. First of all – bullying is aggressive behavior that involves unwanted, negative actions. I can hear that negative voice in your head right now, disagreeing that it's there at all.

Secondly, bullying involves a pattern of behavior repeated over time. Have you ever heard the expression 'practice makes perfect'? It doesn't! Practice makes Permanent. If your inner voice is allowed to continue to practice belittling and criticizing you it will become one of your permanent beliefs. (Unless you work to intentionally change it, which is what you are doing right now).

Finally, bullying involves an imbalance of power or strength. How often do you talk yourself out of things, or tell yourself you're not good enough, smart enough, or good looking enough? Has anyone ever told to you: "Stop beating yourself up over...."

I suggest that many people are bullied by their own subconscious and the worst part is that it continues long after they stopped getting wedgies in Junior High.

Have you ever not begun a project or taken action because you convinced yourself that it was beyond your ability or out of your scope of expertise? Perhaps your inner bully told you that you were too tall, too short, too skinny, too fat, too silly, too stern, or just too plain ol' dumb.

Those thoughts repeatedly assault you with negative and unwarranted ideas and beliefs. They come at you even though you would rather not have them and over time the negative beliefs of your subconscious become the norm.

This is where it truly messes you up, because the thoughts that you think cause you to have certain feelings about yourself. And it's these feelings that determine the types of actions you will take or not take. If your thoughts tell you that you "can" do something then you will most likely give it a shot.

> "Whether you think you can or think you can't - you are right."
>
> Henry Ford

On the other hand, if your bully tells you you're a complete loser and a total dufus and that you're just going to fail and embarrass yourself in the process, then you are much less likely to ever take the chance of moving forward.

To make matters worse, your decision not to act reinforces the Bully Within and you begin to believe your inner bully is right –that you are a loser and a dufus and that your life will never change (because it never does.)

> "We have to learn to be our own best friends because we fall too easily into the trap of being our own worst enemies."
>
> Roderick Thorp

I have a solution for you. It is time for you to kick your own ass! And the sooner the better! It's time for you to stand up to the bully between your ears, be your own hero, and maturely say, "You are not the boss of me!"

Even though the bully of the subconscious mind has been pushing you around for years, it's never too late to push back.

How do you do it?

You do it with your conscious mind. You intentionally choose thoughts that are more empowering, thoughts that move you forward, thoughts that reinforce your value.

Your thoughts are like muscles. The ones you work out the most become the strongest. Bullies only pick on the weak. It's time to start exercising your free will. It's time to start exercising your Positivity Muscles. It's time to intentionally decide that you are totally awesome and that you can do anything. It's time to tell the subconscious that you're not going to take any crap from it anymore.

Remember back a few chapters when I talked about the 5 Keys to Happiness? One of the keys was: Love yourself for who you are right now. I gave you a 10-

minute daily exercise to do each day. All you had to do was simply state positive affirmations about yourself for five minutes in the morning and five minutes at night. It's the perfect defense against The Bully Within.

Did you do it? If yes, are you still doing it?

If so, great! If not, I suggest it is The Bully Within that's holding you back. In fact, I can hear your bully right now. "Those exercises don't help. I feel stupid doing them. I don't have time." Yup, your bully is down-right chatty. If this is the case, decide to stand up for yourself. Be your own hero. Start doing the exercise and quiet that bully once and for all.

> "If you hear a voice within you say 'you cannot paint,' then by all means paint, and that voice will be silenced."
> Vincent Van Gogh

A 10-minute affirmation is just the start to combating The Bully Within and if you found that you didn't even stick to that, then you have even more reason to read on and do this next exercise.

After all, you haven't had an exercise in a while and if you haven't done the others, go ahead and start with this one. It's powerful.

Taken from a process I learned from Zen Master Cherie Huber, this exercise will help you find something much stronger than the venom of your negative-talking inner voice.

Most inner voice yapping is the result of events from your past, which in turn haunt your present. In other words it doesn't take a schoolyard bully to mold your inner voice to speak negatively against you. It could be hidden words or actions from a non-supportive parent when you were a child. In fact, it may even be an event that didn't mean much at the time (because 'kids are so resilient') but has crept into your thoughts in your twenties and won't let go (meanwhile, you're in the higher end of forty). It may possibly have to do with a person that broke up with you unexpectedly, or a friendship that ended badly, or a business that went bad. It's amazing how a few negative events in life can exponentially infiltrate our thoughts and feelings and veer us off course from what we know is true for ourselves.

> "I am convinced all of humanity is born with more gifts than we know. Most are born geniuses and just get de-geniused rapidly."
>
> Buckminster Fuller

A Letter to Yourself Exercise

Here is a way to strengthen your positive mind muscles. You will need a pen, paper, and a recording device of some kind.

1) <u>Choose a person or event</u> with someone that is the culprit behind that bullying voice within. You know the person who made you feel small, dumb or worthless. Maybe it was an interaction that stifled your creativity or stopped you from following your passion.

2) <u>Write a letter to yourself.</u> Write a letter stating all the things you wish they had said, done, or thought about you. Write a letter to yourself regarding the event and how the person who hurt you would have sounded had they stood in support of you. Create a letter that fills your heart with joy, love, empowerment, confidence, creativity, passion, and gratitude.

3) <u>Grab your chosen recording device.</u> Take a few minutes (don't worry about being perfect – that's just another Bully Within trying to stop you from proceeding with this process) and read the letter aloud into the recorder.

4) <u>Throw on some headphones</u>. Lay back (unless you are driving) and take a listen. You are now listening to your best friend and he or she has some AMAZING things to say about you.

5) <u>Put the recording on any number of devices.</u> This is so you can get your hands on it and listen as often as possible. The more you listen to it, the more those positive, loving, wonderfully empowering thoughts will replace the other junk that simply isn't true.

6) <u>Repeat.</u> Repeat this exercise as needed with other bullying memories that need to be replaced with Truth.

"People are like stained-glass windows. They sparkle and shine when the sun is out, but when the darkness sets in their true beauty is revealed only if there is light from within."

Elisabeth Kübler-Ross

Note: Like most bullies, your subconscious is pretty dumb. If you find you are having trouble with this because you can't find anything positive to write about yourself, then make something up! The subconscious doesn't know the difference between real and imagined, so go for it. You have my permission to become the Dr. Seuss of making good stuff up.

An Added Bonus

Look in the mirror and tell yourself that you are amazing and that you can do anything you set your mind to. Don't forget to quote Billy Crystal as Fernando on *Saturday Night Live* and tell yourself, "You look MAAAAAARVELOUSSSS!!"

WARNING The Bully Within will try to tell you that this is stupid and that nothing you say is true. It will try anything to keep you weak. Don't let it. Stick with it. Those muscles of positivity will take time to develop, but they will.

These exercises, if put into regular practice, will quiet that Bully Within; when that happens your life will continue to move from terrible to terrific. Just think how great it will feel to stop giving yourself those mental wedgies.

> "Once you replace negative thoughts with positive ones, you'll start having positive results."
>
> Willie Nelson

The power to turn terrible into terrific is within you. Go back and do the exercises in this chapter –no more excuses.

Your Erroneous Zone

I am sure at times while reading this book and doing the exercises your 'Bully Within' has filled your head with mind-chatter screaming, "But Dennis I can't simply jump from this deep pit I am in to *Terrific* simply by reading and doing the exercises on these pages," or possibly, "What if it doesn't work? I am worried that no matter what I do, my situation will not change."

Oh, but you can.

Remember one of the many great quotes in this book by Henry Ford, "Whether you think you can or you can't, you're right."

Cut yourself some slack. Getting out of your comfort zone takes energy. Celebrate your successes so far.

When you arrived at your moment of decision – to make positive change in your life by reading this book, you took action. You then kept reading. There were exercises that you did (or not) and you found insights offering tools to change your mindset in order to change your life.

Now, it's time to build upon what you've read. Keep moving forward. See, you decide in an instant. Then, you do the work to support that decision, which takes time.

We are setting a longer-term plan in motion. A plan filled with continued insight and positive action steps to help you climb each rung of the ladder in *Turning Terrible into Terrific*. I am sure I've pushed some buttons and have definitely implored you to do some exercises to help make positive change. Check in with yourself to see why you did or didn't do them. Go back if you need to or simply keep reading and soak it all in as you keep moving forward.

The important thing is to shut off that 'Bully Within' that wants to take you out of the process. Don't worry about being right or perfect. Don't worry about the 'what ifs' that may be zipping around your brain. They are not worth it.

When I was a senior in High School many moons ago, I became part of a mentorship program where the upperclassmen guided (or sometimes misguided) the lower classmen. In preparation for this position we had to take a one-day seminar on positive leadership. We were also required to read two specific books. This elaborate training regimen, I believed, was designed purely to prevent us from totally ruining these younger kids' lives. Anyway, I digress.

One of the books I had to read was by Wayne Dyer called *Your Erroneous Zones*. When I saw it on the mandatory reading list I was psyched. I was psyched for two reasons. First, I was 17 years old at the time. Second, I misunderstood the title. However, even though the book had nothing to do with my (or your) erogenous zones, I did learn something that has stuck with me to this day.

I don't remember the exact wording (after all, it wasn't yesterday), but I do remember the lesson. Dyer posed this question to his readers: "What are you avoiding now by using up this moment with worry?"

He then proceeded to offer an example using a variation on the common phrase: 'Don't cry (worry) over spilled milk,' asserting that worry was a waste of time.

You see, if you worry that you might spill the milk and it never spills, then you worried for no reason and if you spill the milk, worrying about it afterwards isn't going to clean it up.

> "Worry is a thin stream of fear trickling through the mind. If encouraged, it cuts a channel into which all other thoughts are drained."
>
> Arthur Somers Roche

Dyer went on to explain that the best antidote for worry was ACTION. In this case, getting a sponge and some paper towels and wiping the table is what was needed to clean up the mess.

It seems that too many people worry about too many things and here's the kicker – most of the things you worry about never even happen. Basically you spend day after day and night after night worrying about things that don't happen and even if your biggest fears come true –all that worrying isn't going to fix it.

> "Don't worry about the world coming to an end today. It is already tomorrow in Australia."
>
> Charles M. Schulz

If you want to turn terrible into Terrific... Stop worrying!

I believe worry is the leading cause of paralysis. It's the way you convince yourself that it's okay to sit on your butt and do nothing. You worry because somewhere deep down a part of you questions whether or not you can handle whatever is coming up in your life. I say it's time to shut off that negativity faucet for good.

Replace any negative thoughts with this simple phrase and watch your life start to change: "I can handle anything that comes my way!"

Now take that with you for the remainder of this book and continue to change your thoughts at the speed of light – one rung of the ladder at a time.

> "Fatigue is often caused not by work, but by worry, frustration and resentment."
>
> Dale Carnegie

Take a breath. *Turning Terrible into Terrific* may take a while.
Worry is not an option and spilled milk will stink, if not cleaned up.

Don't Worry Boss, We'll Handle It

Many years ago, I launched my first entrepreneurial endeavor in the air freight trucking business. With a lot of fire, a little skill and a tremendous amount of naivety, I plunged into the world of business. We were a small company of only about 35 people operating at the LAX International Airport. It was a hearty but motley crew of warehouse workers, drivers, customer service, sales and accounting that were mostly Samoan, Tongan, African-American and Mexican without much formal education or experience.

What we possessed in energy, we clearly lacked in financial acumen at the time. As a result, there were several pivotal moments in our start-up when we reached "death's door." Times when I was convinced the game was over. I recall two specific instances.

About 5:30PM on a Friday evening, which was our busiest night, I got a call from one of the members of our team that we had gotten locked out of the staging warehouse that we used to load our trucks because the landlord had defaulted on their note. This was a major disaster! With no place to receive and load freight, we were out of business!! Customers were calling, frantically demanding that we pick up freight that they had booked for transport. But we had no place to operate. In the short life of our new company it seemed that we were already dead. Customers were screaming at us telling us they would NEVER use us again and that they would spread the word throughout the whole community of our incompetence. It was ugly!! By now it was 7:00PM and everything was in shambles. It was like a battle zone and MASH unit combined. Customer service people were in tears, the phone was ringing off the hook... it was horrible!

At wit's end and in panic, I called the whole team together, told them the situation and with shame and tears in my own eyes, apologized to them and told them they could go home, that we were shutting down and that I would try to find a way to pay them sometime in the future.

When I stopped my blubbering, two of the Samoan warehouse workers stood up and said, "Don't worry boss, we'll handle it!" As I stood there clueless and numb, a swirl of activity ensued. A customer service person ran out of the room and came back to announce that a realtor friend of hers agreed to open a loading dock still under construction that we could borrow for the night even though it was only 10% the size of our normal warehouse. One of the Tongan crew called home and got all of his relatives to drive up to the airport to help out. Someone else got a hold of some mobile phones; others jumped into cars and started driving to customers' offices. Another bunch jumped into trucks, borrowed vehicles and took off to our customers' shipping facilities. (I don't even know if they all had licenses!!!)

By midnight, our crew was blocking major intersections around the airport as they maneuvered the massive fifty foot trailers back-to-back transferring freight from one to another, without the use of a loading dock or forklift, but with the strong backs and willing spirit of the Tongan and Samoan team!!

That night we loaded and shipped over half a million pounds of freight, which was more than five times what we had ever done before! The company never looked back. Even at a time when we suffered the non-payment and loss of over three-quarters of a million dollars in cash owed to us by a factoring company, that same team agreed to work without pay to turn the company around (which we did)... even though I had thought it was over.

The lessons I learned from my team through those experiences about spirit, team, Code of Honor and the power of intention, not only changed my life, but also changed the lives of thousands of people all over the world as I have taught those lessons to others. I learned that you win not on talent, intelligence or charisma. You win when you are surrounded by great people and have a strong Code that holds you together. In that context, when bad things happen, miracles emerge.

Blair Singer

CEO - XCEL Training and Sales Partners Worldwide
Best Selling Author of *Little Voice Mastery, Sales Dogs* and
The ABC's of Building a Business Team That Wins

Mediocrity is a Pain in the Ass

No matter what you are looking to achieve in *Turning Terrible into Terrific*, it's important to realize that even the happiest, most successful people face their own personal fears and doubts on a daily basis. They simply choose not to be stopped by them. That is what makes those people successful. They are willing to take chances. They are decisive, and they prefer to move forward along whatever path will get them to achieving their goals. Of course they prefer the path of least resistance, but will in fact, move regardless of any challenges or obstacles. They do so in spite of any fears or doubts that come up.

> "All growth is a leap in the dark, a spontaneous, unpremeditated act without benefit of experience."
>
> Henry Miller

If you want a Terrific life, at some point in time you are going to have to really go for it – without reservation or hesitation. You are going to have to take a chance on greatness.

> "Be not afraid of greatness: some are born great, some achieve greatness, and some have greatness thrust upon them."
>
> William Shakespeare

Have you ever heard the phrase 'Without risk there is no reward'? Those words really sunk in during a vacation I took with my wife recently.

For our 19th wedding anniversary, my wife Lisa and I decided to spend a weekend on Block Island. We were looking forward to some time to ourselves and had heard about this hidden gem. Full of beautiful beaches, a lighthouse, great views of a large anchorage, incredible history and great restaurants, we thought it would be the perfect place to explore.

Just off the coast of Rhode Island, it turned out – Block Island is a tiny little speck of land. It's so small that we'd seen just about everything we'd wanted to see by five p.m. the day we arrived.

I am not the kind of person who likes to lie around all day, so by the time we finished dinner I was already antsy. I didn't want to ruin things for Lisa but I thought, "What the heck are we going to do tomorrow?"

Luckily, I found one of the local tourist guidebooks in the hotel room and began thumbing through it. I came across an impressive ad with a picture of a group of very beautiful people, sitting atop amazing looking horses, riding peacefully along the surf line of a white sand beach. I though that this was the perfect idea for our second day. After all, Lisa was an avid rider with years of experience. On the other hand, my riding resume consisted of being led around a circle for approximately five minutes, on a pony named Lollipop when I was seven years old. With that under my belt, I was confident in my abilities and immediately picked up the phone to arrange a two-hour beach ride.

We arrived at the Ranch around noon. Two horses were already saddled up and waiting for us. Lisa was shown her horse named Dinero. An experienced rider, Lisa held onto the reigns, put her left foot in the stirrup and mounted her horse with ease.

I was about to mount my horse but apparently, upon seeing how muscular and tall I was, it was determined that I deserved a bigger horse. (Stop laughing; I am at least pretty tall). Our guide, Spencer, called over one of the ranch hands and instructed him to go back into the barn and saddle up 'King' for me. The ranch hand looked me up and down, shook his head and headed off to the barn.

When King emerged from the barn five minutes later, my eyes widened, my jaw dropped, and the little voice inside my head began to question my equestrian abilities (not to mention my sanity). The only time I had ever seen a horse that huge was during a Super Bowl halftime commercial pulling a Budweiser cart. Ignoring the little voice, I stood tall and confident as I clumsily put one foot in the stirrup and mounted King.

Once we were all ready, Spencer led us down the driveway and out to the road. For the few minutes or so, the pace was kept to a casual walk; partly because we were on the road and partly, I think, because Spencer wanted to make sure I wasn't going to fall off!

Once I got comfortable, I looked around to see how far we'd gotten. We'd been riding for about 10 minutes, but only managed a few hundred yards. At this rate, I thought, it was going to be a long two hours and we weren't going to get very far.

That is when I learned my first lesson of the day:

Safety is over-rated and going slow sucks.

Sure you may be slow and comfortable, but you don't really get anywhere and it's really boring. What are you waiting for? In life, going slow and avoiding risk may keep you safe, but it will also keep you almost exactly where you started.

> "A ship in harbor is safe, but that is not what ships are built for."
>
> John A. Shedd

Thankfully, Spencer's confidence in us (and by us, I mean me) increased, and he invited us to pick up the pace. I was really looking forward to doing this. Having never trotted in my life I responded, "Absolutely."

"Okay. Here we go," Spencer made a clicking sound and his horse responded immediately.

Trotting, in case you didn't know, is the equivalent of a slow jog for a horse. It's sort of a middle pace, a mediocre speed for the horse. Not too fast, not too slow.

Like I said, I was looking forward to this.... right up until we started. You see, along with a horse's increased speed comes large amount of quick up and down bouncing movements. Since we were on top of the horses, *we* all also experienced an increase in the up and down bouncing motion. King was the largest of all the horses and as such he bounced up and down more than any of the other horses. Being on top of King, you can imagine, I bounced up and down a bit more than the other riders. Unfortunately, my downs (more often than not) coincided with King's ups – resulting in a very painful union of man and beast.

After a few minutes of this, Spencer turned to look back at us. My wife's hysterical laughter must have drawn his attention. In fact, I think he was barely containing his own laughter as he slowed the horses back down to a walk.

I took a moment to breathe and regain my composure. I was sure we must have ridden a long way as my bottom told me so. However, when I looked back I noticed we hadn't gotten much further than we had walking. That is when I learned my second lesson of the day:

Mediocrity can be a pain in the ass.

When you don't fully commit to going for what you want, you are going to have a lot of ups and downs and you still won't get very far along the path to your goals.

> "There is plenty of room at the top because very few people care to travel beyond the average route. And so most of us seem satisfied to remain within the confines of mediocrity."
> Benjamin Nnamdi Azikiwe

I didn't like trotting. Luckily, I only experienced the ups and down of 'equestrian mediocrity' for a short time. There was nothing comfortable about mediocrity as far as I was concerned.

When we finally turned off the road, Spencer led us down a wooded, sandy path. I could hear the sound of the ocean almost immediately. The brush opened up and we were met by the misty ocean breeze and smooth, white sand that stretched for miles against a cloudless sky.

As we alternated between walking and trotting for the next 10-15 minutes, we marveled at the sailboats in the distance. It was beautiful and it felt great.

At some point I remember my wife calling ahead to Spencer and asking him if it would be okay to let the horses run, and by run she meant gallop.

I distinctly recall Spencer (in all his 19 year-old wisdom) respond, "Umm, I don't see why not."

The little voice inside my head began screaming at me. "Why Not?! Why Not? I told myself... because I am going to kill myself, that's why not!

While my inner voice continued its internal diatribe assuring me that I had no experience, that I would die or at the very least fall off and break my neck, I heard my lips say, "Giddy up!"

I nudged King in the flanks and he shot forward like a bullet. At full speed, King stopped moving up and down so much. Instead, he felt smooth like a train on rails. For the next minute or so, King and I became a synchronous, distance-eating, speed machine. At one point, the wind in my face blew my hat right off my head. It was exciting, scary, exhilarating, rewarding, and fun!

When we finally slowed back down, I caught my breath and I looked back in amazement. King and I covered over half a mile in about 45 seconds. That's when I learned my final lesson for the day:

Go For it!

Commit to your growth. Commit to moving forward. Don't let the little voice inside your head (the one that tells you you can't), stop you from doing the things that can take you where you want to go. You will probably be pleasantly surprised. The fastest path to success is often the smoothest one as well. Sure, you may lose a hat along the way, but you can always go back and get it after you've reached the finish line.

Your dreams are waiting for you. Do yourself a favor, get on your horse, grab the reigns of your life and… Giddy Up!

> "We must walk consciously only partway toward our goal, and then leap in the dark to our success"
> Henry David Thoreau

When it comes to trying new things, how would you describe yourself?

Lagger - preferring to hold back to remain at the end of the line until you were certain that everything would be okay.

Lumper - the 'go with the flow' type of person. Lumped in the pack with the rest of the others. Willing to take action…as long as everyone else is doing it too.

Leader - willing to try new things and to take chances no matter what anyone else says or does.

In my experience almost everyone would love to say that they are a Leader but too few actually live their lives that way. Almost no one wants to be a Lagger, but unfortunately there are more out there than anyone would like.

The biggest group is the Lumpers. This group thrives in the land of mediocrity, feeding on the need for public approval and secretly harboring the desire to blend in with the crowd, to not make waves, to avoid rocking the boat etc….

The Lumpers live in the land of mediocrity. Favorite color: Beige. Favorite food: Milquetoast. Way they like their steak prepared: Medium. The Lumper's life is one of comfort. They have very few lows in their lives but unfortunately even fewer highs. The life of the Lumper is passionless. They justify their choice by pointing out that at least they got in the game unlike the Laggers while at the same time envying the free and vivacious life of the Leaders thereby feeling both satisfied and disappointed at the same time.

I believe that most of us start out as Leaders, willing to take chances. If we didn't we would never have learned to walk. As children we didn't hesitate. We loved trying new things. Back then we had little or no fear about getting in the game, because fear was not natural for us.

Fear is a learned response. And as a result of one's experiences the tendency toward the lagger, lumper, or leader mindset begins to crystallize.

As we grow older, start school, get involved in sports or other activities, we learn vital skills and get encouragement (or not) that can alter or magnify those tendencies.

> "Children are already accustomed to a world that moves faster and is more exciting than anything a teacher in front of a classroom can do."
>
> Major Owens

Later as we enter the dating scene, job market, and evolve socially – we begin to solidify our position as lagger, lumper or leader.

It is important to know where you stand in this triad because the decisions you make about your life are, to a very large extent, determined by your perception of yourself in this hierarchy.

When I use the word leader, it doesn't necessarily mean you have to be a leader of a large group, but in order to turn terrible into terrific – to have a fun, exciting and passion-filled existence – it is critical that you be the leader in your own life. It is imperative that you be willing to "go for it" without waiting for society's approval.

That doesn't mean that you shouldn't take the time to evaluate or weigh your options in decision-making, but eventually taking a leap is required to move forward. Being methodical is one thing, stagnation is another and too much thinking or evaluating can result in inaction or missed opportunities, which result in you never achieving your goal. A leader is thoughtful but is never stopped by what has been described as analysis paralysis.

Lumpers tend to take a chance at moving to the front of the pack only to pull back as soon as it becomes too uncomfortable. You have ups and downs, but never really gain any traction. When things are going well, you feel great, but the slightest downturn and you take yourself out. Over time, you look back at your progress and find you haven't really gotten very far. It's been a long road. Disappointed, but resilient, you keep going and the same pattern occurs and you find yourself right about where you started. It's frustrating and it's slow, yet this is exactly where the majority of people find themselves. For this group, it's three steps forward and two steps back. This behavioral response keeps them in the comfort of the group psyche. It keeps them from being passed but it never lets them get too far out in front either.

> "We learn 10% of what we read, 80% of what we experience, and 95% of what we teach others."
> William Glasser

I recently read something Greg Norman (#1 ranked Professional Golfer during the 80's and 90's) said about the game of golf. He said, "Aggressive play is a vital asset of the world's greatest golfers. However it's even more important to the average player. Attack this game in a bold, confident and determined way and you'll make a great leap toward realizing your full potential as a player."

He did not say study the game, watch others play and judge their performances. In order to turn anything from terrible into terrific, you must study, investigate, or gather information (liking reading this book), then go out and do something with what you learned (like doing the exercises) even when it is uncomfortable. You must also do so with enthusiasm and determination.

In this next exercise you get the chance to take a leap toward stepping out from mediocrity. It is a simple exercise, but not necessarily easy.

Taking a Leap Exercise:

1) Choose something that is beyond your comfort zone.

Choose something you have always wanted to do, but have either been afraid (for whatever reason) to try or simply have not given yourself the time, focus and determination to try. Be sure you know 'why' you want to achieve this, what it is you hope to get out of it and how believe your life will be different once you have accomplished it. These answers will serve as your motivation for sticking it out.

For example:

In your business: i.e., call and ask a mentor or someone of authority for advice on increasing sales

Or personally: i.e., fly on a trapeze or learn how to dance

2) <u>Do something about it.</u>

Example: In the case of getting advice from a mentor – make a list of more than one person in that industry or area of interest. Make a list of questions you'd like to ask. Practice what it is you would say. Begin calling (humbly as well as confidently) until someone says yes to you.

Example: In the case of personally – if you want to learn how to trapeze or dance... don't just sign up for one class, sign up and pay for a package so you can really learn something.

3) <u>Stick it out</u>. Don't come to a screeching halt because something didn't go your way (like losing your hat). It may not be easy in the beginning. Don't think about it. Simply, keep going until you complete the experience.

4) <u>Get the Lesson.</u> Now evaluate. What was your biggest lesson from the experience?

5) <u>Share and Tell.</u> If you are not sure of the learn (lesson), share your experience with others. You'll figure it out. Then encourage others to take the chance on whatever it is they wish to accomplish. You've now led by example without having to be the leader of the pack. Simply Be the leader in your life.

> "Risk more than others think is safe. Care more than others think is wise. Dream more than others think is practical. Expect more than others think is possible. "
>
> Cadet Maxim

Be willing to take chances. Be the leader of your life. Share your experiences. Be willing to laugh at yourself. Don't take life so seriously that you miss the fun.

Ask yourself, "Who am I?"

Coming from a modest, working-class family, I yearned for more than just 'a job'. I didn't know how or what I was looking for, but I left for college with the hopes of transforming my life. For the first time, I felt a sense of true freedom. In my Sophomore year, I met my wife Randi and we decided, almost instantly, that we would start a life together; the house, cars, kids, "the woyks" (as my grandfather would say).

We had our first two children, Chelsea and Lindsey, back to back and needed to feed and clothe our baby girls. Already working 40 hours a week, soon 40 turned to 50 and 50 morphed into 60 hours. I was making "good money" as my mother-in-law would say.

Within a few years, we managed to buy our first house. By the time we welcomed our third (Max) and fourth child (Eden) into our family, I was working 70-80 hours. Barely able to see my family, if the traffic wasn't too bad on the way home, every once in a while I'd get home early enough to read them a bedtime story.

I woke up each day feeling dullness, even dread. I felt no passion in what I was doing at work. I was surely providing for my family but not providing for my soul. I opened my eyes one day and realized more than 10 years had slipped away. My life did not feel like my own any more.

One Saturday morning, while driving with my wife, I pulled over, asked her to take the wheel and said, "Please drive to the hospital." After hours of electrodes, probing and prodding the doctor said, "You are <u>not</u> having a heart attack," and warned me that if I continued with the pace I was going, next time I might not be so lucky.

As we left the hospital, I felt like sobbing. I realized my life was not gone. I didn't die (as I had predicted in my state of fear). I would see my kids grow up. In that instant, I decided things would be very different.

Shortly after that, I began a quest of self-discovery. I felt like I was searching for something. I began reading books like *The Road Less Traveled* by Scott Peck (which was a bit scary at first -- a bit like performing psychoanalysis on yourself), *Awaken the Giant Within* by Anthony Robbins, and *The Power of Constructive Thinking* by Emmet Fox (an amazing spiritual teacher, lecturer and author from the Great Depression era). Then I read a book given to me by another attorney friend called *Secrets of the Millionaire Mind* by T. Harv Eker. In fact, I read it four times! My buddy encouraged me to take three days out of my life and attend a seminar based on the book he'd given me.

Something happened to me (and for me) during that event. I realized that the 'thing' I was searching for wasn't a 'thing' at all (at least it wasn't something outside of myself). It was purpose and fulfillment. I knew like I knew my own name that I needed to take new action in my life, that I needed to search out how I could serve in a bigger way, live as a more enlightened being, and love more fully. I can still feel the exhilaration of that decision nearly 5 years later.

Opportunities began to present themselves to me. I attended another program created by T. Harv Eker called the Enlightened Warrior Training Camp. It was at that life-altering camp that I discovered something that changed my life – I am a leader and learned to own that truth about myself.

As I watched the incredible lead trainer share his gifts to the group and me, I decided that I would follow a similar path. I decided I would become a trainer and positively empower and impact the lives of millions and millions of people around the world. The trainer and I remain friends to this day. His name is Dennis Cummins.

My story of reinvention is pretty wild and is still in progress. It's my belief that we are all reinventing ourselves constantly and if we embrace the reinvention we get to live very full, productive and fulfilling lives. If we resist (as I had done for years), we end up living lives of quiet desperation.

Now when people ask me who I am, I am proud to say I've gone from anxiety-ridden lawyer to exhilarated CEO of one of the largest and most impactful personal and business development training companies in the world -- Peak Potentials Training.

I urge you to stop playing small and encourage you to ask yourself, "Who am I?" Then do whatever it takes to live into it.

Adam Markel – CEO Peak Potentials Training
Author of the soon to be released book
Why Only Live Once - 7 Magical Keys to Reinvent your Life

Ability and Responsibility

There are times in each of our lives when we stumble or fall. From time to time, we all face situations that are challenging or difficult. How you choose to deal with these situations speaks volumes for where you are in your life at the moment.

Most people handle things with a combination of avoidance and denial. The result: they give up or blame someone else for their fate.

But when we choose to face our challenges head-on, learn from our mistakes and choose to continue in spite of them –that is when life becomes Terrific.

Choosing to gallop through life can be exhilarating and may lead to incredible reward. On the other hand, sometimes the speedy route (or taking a leap) may come with a few pitfalls.

Either way, you must be courageous in order to increase your abilities – no matter what it is you are looking to achieve.

In *Turning Terrible into Terrific*, it's about gaining the power or ability to choose to see or do things differently than others. (Hopefully, that includes having an increased sense of humor about it all).

You've probably already noticed that since applying the ideas in this book you no longer view situations, people, or life the same way. You have now become responsible for your own actions. Don't take this lightly because it's something many people are unable to do for themselves.

Additionally, your ability to change your thoughts in an instant are increasing and you now feel empowered to be responsible for your own actions and success rather than getting trapped in the blame game.

That's TERRIFIC.

> "Accept responsibility for your life. Know that it is you who will get you where you want to go, no one else."
>
> Les Brown

Yet, for those moments when you are struggling to grasp any portion of the concepts you've read, I suggest you go back and re-read them. If I've pushed some buttons along the way, go back and see if you can find a different perceptive than the last time you read the section you found disturbing.

Either way it's okay.

> "When you do find humor in trying times, one of the first and most important changes you experience is that you see your perplexing problems in a new way - you suddenly have a new perspective on them."
>
> Allen Klein

I believe we were all put on this earth for a reason. I believe that the universe, higher power, God, great spirit or whatever name you choose to give it would not have put us on this planet without also providing us with the tools and the ability to not only survive but to thrive.

We were also given something amazing – free will. At every opportunity you have a choice of how to respond. You have the ability to decide how you are going to react to any situation or event. You have the choice to use the tools that are available to you or not.

You can choose to say, "I can handle it," or you can say, "Oh crap," and run away.

The fact is that you *can* handle anything that is put in your path. It may not always look pretty (it doesn't have to, by the way), but without exception – know you are equipped to handle anything. The degree of expertise and elegance with which it gets done is something you can work on later.

I'd like to share something that I wrote in my journal on 10/30/2009. Lisa was away on a business trip and I was taking care of Lauren and Chris.

Today is Friday. Lisa has been away all week. Things have gone really well in the house. Lauren continues to be amazing. Today in the morning before school she lost her balance and fell twice.

The first time was downstairs in the entry hall. I was down in the basement sending off the final version of her project, when I heard her fall. When I got upstairs she was on the ground starting to sit up. She was a little upset, but not too bad, when I got there. I asked if she was okay and she said in short clipped speech, "it's okay, I can handle it".

The second time she fell, she was standing upstairs by the bath. After she fell she was very apologetic, "It's my fault."

Earlier I referenced a quote by Henry Ford that I want to revisit. "Whether you believe you can or believe you can't, you are right."

See if you believe you can handle anything that comes your way, you can, and if you believe you cannot handle something, you can't.

After Lauren's fall, the first thing out of her mouth was: "It's my fault". Even though in this case her loss of balance was caused by a dangerously large brain tumor, her 'default mode' was to own her actions.

What's your default mode? Is it to blame others for your fate, is it to ignore situations with the hope that they will go away, or is it to find distractions to delay dealing with the important issues at hand?

The most successful people in business, in finance, in sports, in relationships, in everything are the ones who identify the challenges and obstacles in their environment and face them head on. They either resolve them or, if not resolvable, move past them. Meanwhile most ordinary people are simply stopped by them as if a brick wall was suddenly erected in their path.

When you blame the problem, obstacle or lack of happiness on someone else you are dependent on that someone else to solve it. The problem with that is that the other person may not even consider the situation to be a problem, and even if they did, they may have no interest in solving it for you.

The obstacle that is holding you back is often not even an issue for them. If you want to move beyond what has been holding you back you must take the first critical step. Take responsibility for your part in the situation.

I understand that other people may be involved in it, but if it is affecting you then YOU are involved as well. So ask yourself this question. What role do I play in all this and what do I need to do to move past it?

Are there times when you won't have the skills to solve a particular issue or concern by yourself? Of course there are. But there are also resources out there to assist you in gaining the knowledge to create your own solutions. There are books and seminars and tapes and DVDs and coaches who have the information you have been searching for. But you need to get off your butt and go get the resources you need to be happier and to have the terrific life you deserve and are totally capable of having.

With the right tools and knowledge there is nothing that you can't accomplish. With regard to Henry Ford's quote, I think it needs to be tweaked. The question you need to ask yourself is not whether you can or can't, but whether you will or you won't.

Here is the Dennis Cummins version: "It's never whether you can or can't, it's always whether you will or won't. If you believe you can – you will, if you believe you can't – you won't."

"You cannot avoid the responsibility of tomorrow by avoiding it today."

Abraham Lincoln

 Harness your natural abilities. There is nothing you cannot accomplish. Skills can be learned. It's the right attitude that will propel you.

Eight Degrees Later

My immediate boss and I worked well together, until an unpleasant disagreement. An elderly woman had fallen after tripping on a broken sidewalk outside the building. She had sustained injuries that required medical assistance and wanted compensation, filing a lawsuit against the facility. I'd previously reported my concern over the broken curb. However, the boss's follow-through was delayed due to the expense of repairs.

Following the incident with the elderly woman, I was instructed to write up an incident report giving false information about the exact location of her fall. The goal was to negate the legal responsibilities and nullify the legal case against the organization. I could not do that. It was absolutely against the ethical code my parents taught me and there was no way I could do it with a clear conscience.

My boss demanded I either falsify the report or hand in my resignation.

It was an agonizing decision. Affording a Parochial school education for all three of my children was very important to me. It was a priority. With my youngest, Patty, still in grammar school, my son John in his second year of high school and my daughter, Ann Marie about to graduate with her sights set on attending University, I feared my decision could jeopardize my children's education and future. The income from this job was what I used to pay for their private education. However, despite my fear and uncertainty about my children's futures, I stood my ground and handed in my letter of departure.

It was my oldest daughter, Ann Marie's dream to attend St. John's University. I suggested we visit the campus to see if it was really the place she wanted to be. She confirmed it was and I secretly hoped she would at least receive a partial scholarship. The tuition was way out of my range. Then, something amazing happened.

While touring the campus with my daughter, I spoke with a few of the faculty about possible job openings. That evening I was offered a position on staff. I left the campus knowing that my daughter's full tuition remission benefit was the blessing needed to make it all work. I realize now just how fortunate my family was that ethics won me over. I had stood my ground, in spite of fear, and closed the door to that job.

They say when one door closes another opens...

Ann Marie went on to graduate from St. John's University. So did her sister, Patty. They also both earned their Master's Degrees. My son, John, earned his Bachelor's and I completed my AA, BA and MA!

Twenty-five years later, I remain grateful for the day St. John's University offered me a position on staff.

We all won and I could not be prouder of my children.

Margaret Cashin, Queens, NY

Proud mother of three and grandmother of eight

Chaos is Good

My first year out of Chiropractic school, I worked for Dr. Carmen Campisi. He was the doctor that inspired me to go to Chiropractic school in the first place.

He and I often went out to community events and conducted health screenings as a way of attracting new patients to our practice.

A few months after I had started in his office we acquired a new computerized diagnostic machine called The Metrocom, otherwise known as a digital goniometer. With a rubber-tipped wand attached to a series of swiveling joints, mounted to a stand, and wired to a computer it was used to measure a patient's posture.

We'd place the rubber tip on specific points on a person's body, and then click a button on the wand. The computer would calculate its position in space and give an assessment of the person's postural alignment, which would be displayed on a black and white screen as well as being announced through speakers in a robotic voice that was so bad it made Steven Hawking sound like James Earl Jones.

You're probably thinking that this sounds pretty lame, but 20 years ago this thing was cutting edge!

Shortly after acquiring this state-of-the-art, super-exciting, chiropractic power tool we attended a local Health Fair. We knew there would be about 75 local healthcare providers from various fields and we were anxious to debut The Metrocom. The health fair was scheduled for 11:00 a.m. on a Saturday morning. Every practitioner was given an 8 by 12 ft. space to set up a promotional booth.

We arrived early. After setting up the machine, calibrating the computer, and connecting the speakers, I prepared the sign-up sheets, while Carmen finalized the booth display. By 10:59 we were ready to go.

The doors opened and the hall started to fill with curious locals, who scattered liberally around the various booths.

A moment later, I began my first scan. As I pushed the button on the wand, the computerized voice could clearly be heard over our speakers robotically saying: "Di-gi-tizing A-cro-mi-um Pro-cess"

At 11:01 all hell broke loose!

It was bedlam. A mob of people, who heard the alien voice on the speakers, stormed the booth. It was like a huge vacuum had been created around our booth. It seemed that we had sucked every body in the hall away from the other booths and over to ours. Within minutes there were 40-50 people surrounding us. People were pushing and shoving to the front of the table to get to our sign-up sheet. It was nuts! From that moment, it was impossible to keep up with the sheer mass of people.

After about 45-minutes of non-stop action, with no end in sight, we were falling behind. All the noise and commotion around our booth made it nearly impossible for me to hear the computer issuing the instructions for the next body part to be tagged. At some point, I remember turning to Carmen and saying: "This is terrible, we're getting really backed up"!

To this day I remember his response. He grabbed my

shoulders, looked me in the eye and with a huge grin on his face he said, "Den, chaos is good! Breathe. Look around."

It took me a moment to grasp what he had just said. Scrunching my brow and shaking my head I silently questioned, "Chaos is good?" It made no sense. We were totally understaffed and completely overwhelmed. We were out of control. How could chaos possibly be good?

> "Chaos is inherent in all compounded things. Strive on with diligence."
>
> Buddha

I looked around the auditorium. All the other booths were calm and orderly. None of the other practitioners had unruly mobs at their booths. None of the other Doctors were as harried, overwhelmed and worn out as we were. None of the other practitioners were as backed up as we were. Everyone else looked calm and maybe just a little bored.

That's when the brilliance of those three simple words hit home. Those three simple words taught me one of my greatest lessons about business, about success and about growth.

Our booth may have been unruly. Our booth may have been overcrowded. And our booth was definitely in a state of chaos, but we were busy. Very, very busy! In fact, we had the only busy booth at the entire event and that was the purpose for being there in the first place.

We saw more people in that one Saturday afternoon than we had seen our last six previous events combined and as a result of that day our practice grew 17% the next month.

Chaos is good!   Chaos is exciting. Chaos can be profitable and chaos can lead to growth.

> "Chaos is a friend of mine."
>
> Bob Dylan

The key is to tap into and harness the energy created by the chaos, without actually getting caught up in it. It's important that you be willing to let go of your need to control all the events that are going on around you. Let's face it things rarely go exactly as planned. The point is to be flexible and go with the flow. Especially when the way you thought it would go turns out to be even better than expected!

Sometimes the mere fact that you are the only calm one in the situation puts you in a position of authority and gives you the chance to demonstrate your leadership skills. Most people agree that they make much better decisions when they remain calm in the midst of chaos.

> "In the midst of movement and chaos, keep stillness inside of you."
>
> Deepak Chopra

Chaos also forces you to think outside the box. After all, if it were inside the box, it wouldn't be chaos. And all growth occurs when you stretch beyond your comfort zone. Embrace chaos as an opportunity to experience something new and to develop new skills as a result.

The easiest way to avoid frustration and the sense of being overwhelmed is to simply accept the fact that there are moments in life when you have no control over events and situations. Instead of getting sucked into those situations and becoming part of the chaos, simply choose to take a step back and ask yourself how the situation can be used to your advantage.

> "No chaos, no creation. Evidence: the kitchen at mealtime."
>
> Mason Cooley

Expect the unexpected. Be ready for anything and always look for what's working for you in any situation. Even in chaos there is order. It's usually just harder to find. By planning for chaos you decrease your level of anxiety and when you are calmer your decision-making ability is clearer.

It's easy to get caught up in the emotions of the moment if you are not prepared. I am not suggesting that you can always be ready for every contingency, but you can at least plan on how you will react when the unexpected occurs. Knowing that you are ready for anything gives you confidence. Confidence will increase your ability to take positive actions.

Chaos is a good thing. Enjoy It!

> "If you can keep your wits about you while all others are losing theirs, and blaming you... The world will be yours and everything in it..."
>
> Rudyad Kipling

Let go of your need to control everything.
Expect the unexpected. Remain calm.
Chaos is good.

Preparing for Chaos

There are times that feel chaotic in our growing small business, DeepStream Designs, Inc. We started the company in 2006 to design and manufacture high-end custom planters and recycling bins for hospitality, commercial and residential projects. Tom was inspired to create our original Mariner planter when we were sitting at a sidewalk café in Italy, and he noticed the deteriorating wooden planters along the street. He loved the classic design of the planters, and as he looked at the rotting planks, he started sketching on a napkin his idea for a planter that would stand the test of time and literally weather the storms using sustainable design principles he learned rebuilding yachts. Therefore, customers would not have to replace them every few years. We managed to grow our business through the midst of the Great Recession, and the two of us are still the heart of our business, with the help of one production worker.

'Chaos' can be exciting! For example, in the summer of 2010, after surviving a devastating lull in business, all hell broke loose. We received two of our largest orders ever from high-profile customers, and both required that their orders be filled in the same two-month period. That may not sound like a big deal, but those two orders made up 45% of our sales that year! Over night, our production was pushed to its limit, requiring long hours and additional hiring to keep up. Our work area was jam-packed. Every day felt like a game of Tetris, as Tom moved materials around to make everything fit in what had recently seemed like a very large 10,000 square foot manufacturing space.

In the end, we nearly doubled our sales in 2011. We also secured our ability to keep our skilled employee full-time at a living wage, and to hire additional workers when necessary.

We believe the key to benefiting from the chaotic times is being proactive and planning for all eventualities, including success! We developed tools that systematized the handling of our business *before* we were 'found' by the big guys, and we took advantage of low rents during the recession to move into a space that was six times the size at just double the rent so we could grow into our ever-increasing business. Tom invested in tools that would improve production efficiency, so we could make more with fewer people. We even purchased manufacturing accounting software that large businesses use to manage inventory and costing.

Our business is somewhat seasonal, so during slower times we discipline ourselves to work on marketing and "housekeeping" tasks, putting systems in writing, and streamlining production – all of which is important to our continued success, but is put off when business is booming.

Most importantly, we don't allow the feeling of being overwhelmed to paralyze us. However chaotic things feel, we realize it is just a state of mind. Having created a solid foundation, we welcome the 'chaos'. Each time it's upon us, it means we have reached a new level in the growth of our business, and that is a great feeling!

Sheila and Tom Boyce
Owners – DeepStream Design

Are you Smarter than a 5th Grader?

For the past several years I've had the opportunity to watch more episodes of Jeff Foxworthy's show titled "Are you smarter than a 5th Grader?" than I care to admit. Over that time, two things have become abundantly clear to me.

First, Jeff Foxworthy has a terrible haircut (members of the Foxworthy Fan Club can leave their complaints, or kudos, regarding my keen sense of observation, at www.TurningTerribleIntoTerrific.com where they will most likely be completely ignored). Secondly, over 90% of the people who think they are smarter than a fifth grade are in fact, not.

That means that if you're hanging out with nine other people at a party and you're trying to figure out who amongst you is smarter than a 5th Grader, there's a 90%

probability that it ain't you.

Does that mean you still secretly harbor the desire to eat worms and pull girls' pigtails or that you're incapable of functioning in an adult society? Of course not! Besides, most adult women don't wear pigtails and worms are actually an excellent source of protein.

Does it mean that you are unable to function in your job, profession and most social situations due to the fact that you can no longer recall all 13 of the original colonies? Of course it doesn't! (Just so you know, for your next holiday party, they are: NH, MA, RI, CT, NY, NJ, PA, MD, DE, VA, NC, SC, and GA).

However, it does mean that over 90% of the population thinks they are smarter than they actually are.

In my experience, most people reach a certain point in their educational career at which they declare defiantly to the academic gods: "I'm done!" After all, just how long did they expect you to stay in school?

It may have been a perfectly rational decision back then. Other priorities became more apparent; like getting a job, start a family, or do some traveling. You may have even thought about returning to school at some point or considered taking a continuing education class from time to time, but simply never did. Life eventually got in the way and you let it go. Until, however, reading this book (or something else) you realized how important it is to keep learning and growing.

The mind is like a muscle—when you exercise, it becomes firmer and stronger. When you stop exercising it becomes flabby and soft. That is why I've had you do exercises and take action steps while reading this book. Otherwise you are simply coasting.

To stay sharpest and hold onto what you have learned, it is important to keep expanding upon these new (or reminded) lessons. You must continue to exercise your mind.

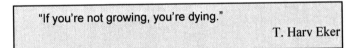

"If you're not growing, you're dying."
T. Harv Eker

It is important to really take a good hard look at what actions you are taking in your life to move yourself forward toward your goals. Not just your intellectual goals, but your spiritual, physical, financial, emotional and interpersonal goals. To have a Terrific life it is important that you continue to develop all of these facets of your life.

Too often, people become complacent about their growth. At some point they decide that they are done, not only with school, but also with growth in general.

At some point they decide that life is 'good enough'. But, as you've read, mediocrity can be a pain in the ass. Continued growth is the true path to happiness.

> "Without continual growth and progress, such words as improvement, achievement, and success have no meaning."
>
> Ben Franklin

'Good enough' is what you say when whatever it is you've attempted didn't turn out the way you had hoped or desired. It's what you say when you realize the picture you just hung on the wall is 1/8 inch lower than the one next to it. It's what you say when your meal at the restaurant comes to the table and it's not exactly what you had ordered. But rather than have them correct it and get what you REALLY want, you settle. It's what you say to yourself after you've committed to losing 25 pounds but stop after losing 10, having managed to fit into the jeans you had hanging on the back of the door as motivation. It's what you say to yourself about your passionless relationship with your partner. It's what you say to yourself about the job you hold that leaves only a few dollars in your wallet after you pay the bills each month. And it's the phrase you use to describe any aspect of your life that has fallen short of your dreams.

The tricky thing is that 'good enough' is often quite comfortable. When your life is good enough there is very little pain, and often nothing to even complain about. That's why so many people are willing to settle for it. On the down side, there is also very little excellence, passion or joy and often nothing to ever celebrate.

'Good enough' condemns you to a comfortable life of mediocrity. 'Good enough' is the killer of dreams.

What I am about to say may offend some of you, but I want to be perfectly clear on this point: "Good Enough'...sucks!

'Good Enough' has two foundational causes: lack of action and/or lack of knowledge. In the first case, it's not that you don't understand what it would take to improve your situation, but rather that you consciously or unconsciously choose not to take those actions and to remain in a state of stagnation. This is usually done out of fear: fear of the unknown, fear of change, fear of what others might think, etc., etc. You know there is something better out there and you know what it would take to have it, but you can't seem to take the next step to get it done and it is crippling you from achieving happiness in that area.

Instead, you say things like: "I could have that, or do that, or be that, if I wanted to"… but you never do this, that or the other thing because not taking action allows you to avoid the risk of failing and possibly embarrassing yourself. Not taking action also allows you to avoid the risk of succeeding and the discomfort sometimes associated with change or even success. By neither failing nor succeeding you solidify that safe and comfortable existence in the land of 'good enough'.

The second cause of remaining in a state of 'good enough' is not about your willingness to take action, but in knowing what action to take. Maybe you've even tried several different actions, possibly in many directions. In fact, you want so badly to move beyond 'good enough' that you are willing to try any new thing that comes your way.

Frequently disappointed that the latest fad didn't

deliver the results you had hoped, you still continue to throw yourself into anything and everything without a plan, but with the hope that somehow something will stick. The problem is you just don't know what is needed to move you closer to your goal. This is what happened to me after I graduated Chiropractic school. I was eager, I was motivated, and I was willing to try just about anything. Consequently that is what I got: Just about anything. My business was all over the place. It had no true direction. For every step forward it seemed I took two steps back. My problem wasn't that I wouldn't act. It was that I didn't know what to do or when to do it. I knew a lot about chiropractic care, but I knew very little about running a chiropractic business. As a result, my business struggled. I struggled and my family struggled. I continued to struggle until I found a mentor and a coach to show me the ropes and teach me what to do. Dr. Carmen helped me to focus on the things that would really make a difference in the success of my practice. Once I knew what to do, my practice soared.

No matter which group you fall into, if your life is not as Terrific as you would like it to be there is only one reason why.

There's something you <u>don't</u> know!

> "The only thing more expensive than education is ignorance."
>
> Benjamin Franklin

Either you don't know what to do next or you don't know what's preventing you from doing the next thing. Let's face it, if you knew what to do to turn your life from terrible into terrific or from good to great – you would have done it already. If you knew what was holding you back from taking action, you would have acted already.

What it basically comes down to is that there is a big difference between information and application. To be truly successful in all aspects of your life, you need both. That is why it is vitally important that you not only continue to learn, but also apply what you have learned.

For those of you who are not sure what to do next, it is critical that you continue to expand your knowledge base. The biggest challenge you may face in moving to the next level is your own environment: the environment at home; the environment at work; the environment between your own ears; the environment that drags you down and the environment that is not supportive of your growth.

My Suggestion: Find someone to help you stay focused. Surround yourself with like-minded people. Find a way to stay motivated and inspired.

If you want to make it easier on yourself, find a role model to follow. Over the past 30 plus years I have had the great fortune to have been exposed to some incredible role models like Wayne Dyer, Tony Robbins, T Harv Eker, and Brian Tracy. But before them, there was Jules Schwartz, the 90 year old holocaust survivor who lived down the hall from us in our apartment building who taught me about perseverance; my wife Lisa who continues to encourage me to stretch myself; and Dr. Carmen Campisi who taught me that success and fun were not mutually exclusive. I have been inspired by them and continue to learn from their examples.

> "I've learned that people will forget what you said, people will forget what you did, but people will never forget how you made them feel."
>
> Maya Angelou

In my experience most successful people are happy to share their knowledge with those who want it. Find them and learn from them.

If you do what they do, you can have what they have. But first, you must be open to listen and then you must take action.

> "The fact that I can plant a seed and it becomes a flower, share a bit of knowledge and it becomes another's, smile at someone and receive a smile in return, are to me continual spiritual exercises."
>
> Leo Buscaglia

Don't let your new excitement succumb to what my friend Dr. Patrick Gentempo describes as the 'Jacuzzi Effect'. Let me explain. When you are actually in the hot tub the water is all nice and warm and the bubbles feel great on your skin – everything feels really Terrific. Unfortunately, sooner or later you have to get out of the tub. As soon as you leave the warm embrace of the bubbling water, you become exposed to the environment. The warm relaxed feeling you had in the hot tub begins to fade and you start to feel a chill as goose bumps begin to form. That is the Jacuzzi Effect.

This book has been your personal Jacuzzi, and now that you are ready to move on, the real world is waiting. Get ready for the goose bumps and have a warm blanket near by. Change is simple but it isn't always easy. Realize that while the decision to change occurs in an instant, the process of change may take a lifetime.

I hope that I have been able to inspire and empower you to be better than you were yesterday, to achieve your desires and to create a wonderful life for yourself and your loved ones.

If you have gotten this far in the book, you have come a long way towards creating a Terrific life for yourself. Congratulations!

But that's not 'good enough'. This book is a great start in reprogramming your mind for success, joy, achievement, and happiness but it is just the beginning. To help you stay focused on your path to a terrific life, to help you avoid the "Jacuzzi Effect" I have a special surprise for you.

> "One of the greatest discoveries a man makes, one of his great surprises, is to find he can do what he was afraid he couldn't do."
>
> Henry Ford

If you are committed to *Turning Terrible into Terrific* then I am committed to supporting your growth. As my gift to you: simply go to DennisCummins.com and click on the T2T icon to receive weekly inspirations, real world coaching and success strategies. However, don't expect 52 weeks of fluffy kittens, platitudes and quotes 'cause that's not 'good enough'. What you can expect is a weekly dose of success reality that I know will keep you excited about your potential. You'll also receive some real world advice to keep you moving forward. My goal is to entertain you enough to keep you learning and inspire you enough to enable you to achieve the life you have always dreamed. I'm here to help.

The information is there for you. All you need to do is: <u>Take Action!</u>

Simply go to:
DennisCummins.com/gift/
click on the T2T icon to enroll.

Success is not hard. Having a Terrific life doesn't need to be difficult. You don't need to be a Nobel Laureate to be happy. You don't need to hold a PhD to be successful. You don't even need to be smarter than a 5ᵗʰ Grader in order for *Turning Terrible into Terrific.*

> "If you think education is expensive, try ignorance"
> Ben Franklin

Having a Terrific life doesn't have to be difficult. Find a role model to allow. Never stop being open to learning and growing.

Terrible or Terrific?

I remember the instant my life forever changed. It was 2:37 pm on Tuesday December 22nd 1992.

I was 28 years old. I had graduated Chiropractic school and gotten married just a few months earlier. I had recently purchased my very first "new" car, a 1992 Honda Accord sedan. I had begun working as a chiropractor with my good friend and mentor Carmen, as well as doing home visits with my own patients. I had my health (although I was about 16 lbs heavier than I would have liked). I had nice clothes. I was able to take vacations and travel occasionally. By all outward appearances, my life looked pretty awesome.

It should have been the greatest, most amazing and incredible time of my life, but it wasn't. Don't get me wrong; it wasn't tragic either.

It should have been, would have been and could have been absolutely terrific – if not for one, not-so-small detail. You see... for the previous 12 years I had worked really hard at perfecting the skill of closet alcoholism. Over those 12 years I was able to convert my recreational use of alcohol into a mind numbing, soul-robbing daily addiction.

Despite having all the trappings of wealth on the outside, I was morally, physically and spiritually bankrupt on the inside. It didn't happen all at once. Instead, it consisted of a decade long series of withdrawals from my personal accounts of self-esteem, self-worth, and self-dignity. The 'terrific' things happening on the outside seemed to only temporarily offset the terrible things I was feeling on the inside. Eventually, my life was barely tolerable. It was just 'good enough' and 'good enough'... sucked –big time!

I had tried to stop drinking on my own many times. Each time unsuccessfully. Each failed attempt seemed to solidify my self-loathing and total lack of self-esteem. It was during one of those failed attempts that brings us to the afternoon of Tuesday December 22nd, 1992.

It was a cold blustery gray day. I was five weeks into my latest attempt at sobriety. I showed up at 2:30 p.m. sharp for my weekly alcoholism recovery session. I was sitting across the desk from Judith, my counselor, in a cramped, stuffy, cluttered, six-by-eight foot windowless room. I was hot. I was uncomfortable. I was also... drunk.

It took Judith all of about three minutes to realize that something was not right. She excused herself from the room. At 2:35 she returned with a Breathalyzer machine. At 2:36 I tested positive for alcohol in my system.

She immediately asked me for my car keys and told me that I could no longer participate in the program. She placed two sheets of paper side-by-side on the desk in front of me. One was a list of phone numbers for local taxis to take me home; the other was a list of inpatient rehab centers. Then, without any emotion in her voice, she uttered one word... "Choose."

At 2:37 p.m. on Tuesday December22, 1992 my life changed at the speed of thought.

I chose Rehab.

For someone who had spent the past decade doing everything possible to appear perfect, successful and in control – this was no small decision. Choosing rehab meant choosing to face the shame and embarrassment I felt about my condition. Choosing rehab meant allowing people to see on the outside, what I'd been hiding on the inside. I was terrified, but I chose rehab anyway.

Even though I didn't know or feel it at the time; in that moment, I had also chosen self-dignity, self-esteem, true happiness and, for the first time in longer than I could remember –I would find inner peace.

While the decision to change happened at the speed of thought, as with anything in life; the actual change would progress at the speed of life and as is the case with most changes in our lives; it took the help of some incredible mentors and supporters.

After 30 days of inpatient rehabilitation and expert counseling, the people who understood what I was going through (and who knew what they were talking about), suggested I attend 365 consecutive days of group support meetings. I chose to do that.

I was encouraged to stay in frequent contact with someone who had been through what I was about to go through. I chose to do that, too. The strategy of following in the footsteps of those who had already achieved what I was seeking to master has continued to serve me well. I believe that strategy will serve you well also.

I came to appreciate how critical it is to take responsibility for all my actions and the results they produced, both good and bad.

Until you are willing to accept the fact that everything you like and don't like about your life are the direct results of the decisions you have made in the past, nothing will change for you in the future.

I learned the importance of appreciation and of being grateful for everything in my life. Even in the terrible things that can happen in life something positive can be found. For example, dealing with my daughter's brain tumor has taught me the meaning of family and the importance of living in the moment.

I have continued to develop my ability to focus on what I truly want in my life and then take the actions necessary to achieve them. I make every effort not to get caught up in distractions and work hard to remain focused. However, as with anything, there is always room for improvement. For instance, if I had mastered my powers of focus, this book might have been completed two years earlier than it was.

It has been almost 20 years since that day in Judith's office. If there has been one constant in my life since that day, it would be my dedication to continuing on my path of personal growth.

I understand that I don't know everything (apparently my father was right after all) and there is always room to grow. I am always looking for new ways to expand myself so that I can have even more joy, love and prosperity in my life. I continue to read inspirational books, listen to CDs or attend new courses – not because I don't know enough, but because I want to learn more. I do this not just for me, but also so I may share what I have learned. In fact, sharing what I have learned has become my passion.

Life is the sum total of your decisions, but your past does not have to dictate your future. At any point, you can change the direction of your life by choosing a new path. It happens at the speed of thought. It happens in an instant and, in that instant, you have a choice...

Terrible or Terrific?

You Decide.

$T2^T$

A Note from Dennis

Congratulations! You did it! However, if you make reading this book the last thing you ever do in the quest for your terrific life, I will personally come to your house and punch you in the arm! Okay, I wouldn't do that. But hey, don't let this be the end. You're smarter than that! As great as you think the information in this book is... it is only a start.

I encourage you to continue *Turning Terrible into Terrific*. Simply go to:

DennisCummins.com/gift/

There you will find bonus gifts, including access to the T2T membership site where, each month, there will be a webcast offering continual information, encouragement and answers to your questions. In addition, there will be ongoing exercises to help you master even more strategies for keeping your life in the "terrific zone".

It's simple. If you haven't taken action already, Do it now! Click or go to the link above to access your gifts immediately.

Remember, You are the one responsible for your dreams and happiness. I am here to empower you in making them a reality.

Once again, congratulations for taking action. I look forward to hearing of your continued success and sharing with you on the T2T membership site.

To your Terrific Life,

Acknowledgements

While I am always thankful for the small things in life, the creation of this book was no small thing. It is the culmination of a lifetime of learning and the collaboration of some truly amazing people. I am profoundly grateful for each and every one of you.

I especially want to thank my son Christopher. His creativity, maturity, kindness, and terrific sense of humor make me proud to be his father each and every day.

Special thanks to my wife Lisa for always believing in me and supporting me. Thank you for helping me become the man I am.

Thank you to my daughter Lauren for showing me on a daily basis that happiness is a choice no matter what life hands you.

To my Mom and Dad, Thank you for teaching me the meaning of unconditional love.

My endless gratitude goes out to Kathleen Beales whose tireless efforts and enduring patience made this book possible.

Thanks to Shane Voss and Alannah Avelin for making the book look so fantastic!

My gratitude goes out to Lennie Appelquist, Elizabeth LaPrade, and Bob Haselton who have been instrumental in helping me share my message with the world.

Thank you to all the individuals that shared their stories in this book so others could see that anything is possible.

My thanks go out to all the teachers in my life who have helped mold me into who I am, including Wayne Dyer, Tony Robbins and especially T. Harv Eker who has given me the opportunity to live my passion.

Finally, thanks to all of my dear friends for your honesty, support and encouragement. I Love you!

☺ ☺

Dennis Cummins is an internationally acclaimed speaker, trainer and coach. His quick-witted, straight-talking, no-nonsense style offers an entertaining dose of reality with heart.

Despite his usually cheerful disposition, Dennis has not been immune to dealing with his own personal and professional difficulties. However he has realized that with any challenge, it's not what happens to you in life, but rather the attitude you take and how you respond to it.

After graduating from NY Chiropractic College in 1992, Dennis opened his first of two successful practices on Long Island, NY. Dr. Cummins credits his success to his willingness to continue to learn, great mentors and his knack for finding the positive in any situation. His strong belief in continuing education and coaching led him to become involved in the self-development industry.

Dennis' family is very important to him. He lives on Long Island, with his wife Lisa and 2 children, Christopher and Lauren.

To learn more about Dennis, visit:

DennisCummins.com

If you have a *Turning Terrible into Terrific* story and wish to share, post it on our community site at:

DennisCummins.com

Like us on: T2TCommunity

Follow us on: T2TCommunity

It would be wonderful to hear your honest feedback about your experience with Turning Terrible into Terrific and incredibly appreciated if you shared with others.
Please post an honest review at:

or post on the community site once you've registered at:
DennisCummins.com

I'd be thrilled. Thanks!